The Wondering Place

WHERE KIDS EXPLORE THEIR BIGGEST QUESTIONS ABOUT GOD, JESUS, AND CHRISTIANITY TO BUILD A FAITH THAT LASTS

Jackie Burns

Illustrated by
Lynsey Wilson

Published by **The Holy Hideaway**
www.theholyhideaway.com

Library of Congress Control Number: 2026902882

ISBN 979-8-9933762-1-9 (Paperback)
ISBN 979-8-9933762-3-3 (Hardcover, Case Laminate)
ISBN 979-8-9933762-0-2 (Hardcover, Dust Jacket)
ISBN 979-8-9933762-2-6 (eBook)

First Edition

Dedication

For Emery and Harleigh,

My little angels, you ask the toughest questions and never settle for answers that leave you wondering. Your curiosity, bold hearts, and the joy you bring to others are gifts that make the world a better place. Always follow what is good and true, shine the light of Jesus everywhere you go, and remember every day how deeply you are loved by God.

This book is for you and for every child who is on a journey to know God more. It's for anyone with questions and a heart that wants to understand.

Keep exploring God's goodness, keep growing in faith, and never let go of Jesus.

"You will seek me and find me
when you seek me with all your heart."
— Jeremiah 29:13

Table of Contents

For Parents

Dear Parents,

Welcome to *The Wondering Place*. By opening this book with your child, you're giving them more than answers. You're helping to lay a foundation of faith that can guide and strengthen them for the rest of their life. Children at this age are naturally curious and eager to explore big questions. They deserve clear, truthful answers, and it's a gift to walk alongside them as they learn.

My prayer is that the conversations sparked by this book don't end on the last page. As your child grows up in a world filled with distractions and mixed messages, you can be their steady guide, reminding them of what is true and eternal. Point them often to Jesus, for He is the way, the truth, and the life. Encourage them to trust that God's love will never let them down.

You don't need to have every answer. What matters most is creating an open, ongoing conversation where your child knows they're safe to bring their questions, doubts, and discoveries to you. When you pray together, explore Scripture side by side, and live out your own faith with honesty, your child sees what it means to trust God in real life.

I've done my best to write each chapter from a literal understanding of the Bible and a sincere desire to stay faithful to God's Word. But please don't take my interpretation as the final authority. Let Scripture itself guide your heart, shape your understanding, and be your ultimate source of truth and wisdom.

May this book spark a lifelong journey of faith for your child, one rooted in Scripture and filled with the unfailing love of Christ.

With gratitude and hope,

Jackie Burns

Introduction

Have you ever had a question about God that no one could answer? Maybe you've wondered if God is really out there, why He lets bad things happen, or if He still loves you when you mess up. If you've ever felt curious, confused, or even doubtful about God, you're not alone. Lots of people, even adults, ask those same questions.

That's exactly why this book was written. It's for curious minds like yours. Through these pages, you'll explore some of the biggest questions kids have about God, Jesus, the Bible, and the world around us. You'll find clear answers, real stories, and learn what the Bible teaches about who God is and how much He loves you.

You don't need to have perfect faith to read this book. You can start right where you are, no matter what's on your mind. God isn't bothered by your questions. In fact, He welcomes them. God promises to be close to anyone who seeks Him. He wants you to know Him, trust Him, and see that His love for you is real and never-ending.

I hope that by the time you finish this book, you'll be confident in who God is, trust His Word, and know that His love for you will never fail.

Before we dive into the big questions, please take a moment to read the next section. It explains the most important message you will ever hear, the good news about Jesus, also called the Gospel. This is the reason you can have a real, forever relationship with God.

The Good News About Jesus

The Bible tells us that God made the world and everything in it, including you! He made you to know Him, have a relationship with Him, and live with Him forever (John 17:3).

But all of us have sinned by disobeying God's commands and going our own way (Romans 3:23). Sin separates us from God, and the Bible says that "the wages of sin is death" (Romans 6:23). That means our sin earns a serious punishment. It breaks our relationship with God, and if nothing is done, that separation lasts forever. On our own, there's nothing we can do to fix it.

But because God loves us so much (Romans 5:8), He sent His Son, Jesus, on a rescue mission to save us from sin and bring us back to Him. Jesus came to Earth as God in human form. He is fully God and fully human (Colossians 2:9). He was born as a baby and lived a perfect life without sin, showing us what God is like. Then He willingly gave His life as a sacrifice on the cross, taking upon Himself the punishment we deserved for our sin. Three days later, God raised Him from the dead, showing that Jesus has power over sin and death (1 Corinthians 15:3–4).

Now, because of what Jesus did for us on the cross, everyone who chooses to trust Him as their Savior is completely forgiven of their sins, made right with God, and given the gift of eternal life (John 3:16). This isn't something we can earn. It's a gift God gives us because of His grace (Ephesians 2:8–9).

Following Jesus means He becomes your Lord and Savior, and you belong to Him forever (John 10:27–28). You can talk to Him anytime, learn from His Word, and live with purpose, peace, and joy in Him.

This is the best news you will ever hear, and it's for everyone who chooses to trust and follow Jesus.

Part 1

Evidence That God Is Real

Chapter 1

Is God Real? How Can We Be Sure?

Imagine finding a really cool bird's nest. It's built so perfectly, with each twig and feather in just the right place. You know a clever bird made it, even if you can't see the bird. The world around us is just like that nest, so full of incredible design and beauty that it points to a clever Creator, even if we can't see Him (Romans 1:20).

Let's look at more clues that show us there must be a God.

The World Is Wonderfully Designed

Think about how leaves grow from trees, the fine details of a spider's web, or the colorful wings of a butterfly. Our world is filled with fascinating, detailed creations.

Science tells us that all things, from leaves to spider webs to butterfly wings, are made up of tiny building blocks called atoms that fit together perfectly.

It's like the whole world works as a giant, complicated machine. Just like a machine needs someone to design it, the world needs someone to make it.

The Bible says:

> "The heavens declare the glory of God;
> the skies proclaim the work of his hands."
> — Psalm 19:1

Everything we see in nature points to God's existence.

Our Inner Compass

Have you ever felt bad after doing something wrong, even if no one else knew? Or have you felt good after helping someone? Maybe you stood up for a friend who was being left out and it made you feel good inside.

These feelings are part of our conscience, an inner sense of right and wrong. Our conscience is like a guide written on our hearts, showing us how we should treat others (Romans 2:15).

It's hard to explain this inner compass unless it was placed there by Someone greater than us. God gave us this sense of right and wrong because He wants us to live good, loving lives.

The Bible Tells God's Story

One of the biggest clues that God is real is the Bible itself. The Bible isn't just a history book. It's a collection of sacred writings that show how God has interacted with people throughout time.

Through its pages, we learn about real experiences, real events, and how God has guided, loved, and taught people over thousands of years.

One amazing discovery happened in 1947. A young shepherd exploring near the Dead Sea in Israel found clay jars hidden in a cave. Inside the jars were scrolls that had been untouched for close to 2,000 years. Over the next decade, archaeologists and local searchers found more than 900 scrolls and thousands of tiny pieces of old writing. Almost every book in the Old Testament (the first part of the Bible) was represented, including a complete copy of the book of Isaiah, written long before Jesus was born. Although a few small edges were damaged over time, nearly the entire scroll is still readable.

These scrolls are now called the Dead Sea Scrolls, and they contain some of the oldest copies of the Bible ever found.

When scholars compared them to the Bible we read today, they found the words were almost exactly the same.

This shows how God has protected His Word over time and kept His message of truth and hope safe for us.

Jesus Was a Real Person and the Son of God

Many people wonder, *If God wants us to believe in Him, why doesn't He just reveal Himself?*

But the truth is, He already did.

God came to us in the most real and personal way possible, through His Son, Jesus. Jesus wasn't just a teacher or a kind man. He was fully God and fully human, and He really lived on Earth. He was born as a baby in Bethlehem, grew up in a regular family, and spent His days learning, working, and living life just like us.

He wasn't made up like a fairy tale. He was a real person in history who healed the sick, comforted those who were hurting, and showed us that God is gentle, powerful, patient, and overflowing with love.

But not everyone welcomed Him. Many people rejected Him. In the end, Jesus was beaten and killed. But death didn't win. Three days later, He came back to life (1 Corinthians 15:3–4), proving that God's power is real, and stronger than anything, even death.

The Bible tells us all about the amazing things Jesus did, but it's not the only ancient book that talks about Him. Many people outside the Bible, including Josephus (a Jewish historian), Tacitus (a Roman historian), and Pliny the Younger (a Roman governor), also wrote about Jesus in their historical records. These men weren't Christians, but their writings confirm that Jesus lived, was crucified, and had followers who truly believed He rose from the dead. These ancient sources help us know that Jesus wasn't part of a pretend story. He was a real person who changed the world.

Lives Changed by God

Throughout history, people have shared how God has changed their lives. They talk about finding peace in scary moments, strength when they needed help, and a new sense of purpose they didn't have before. It's like they discovered a treasure in God and now want to share it with others.

The Bible tells us:

> "Therefore, if anyone is in Christ,
> the new creation has come:
> The old has gone, the new is here!"
> — 2 Corinthians 5:17

That's why so many people say they feel transformed, like they've been made new on the inside.

We see this kind of life change all over the Bible. Zacchaeus went from being a greedy tax collector to a generous man who followed Jesus (Luke 19:1–10). Mary Magdalene was set free from a broken and troubled past and became one of Jesus' most faithful followers (Luke 8:1–3). The apostle Peter went from denying Jesus three times to boldly preaching the

Gospel, even when his life was in danger (Luke 22:54–62; Acts 2:14–41).

And that kind of change still happens today. People around the world continue to experience God's love in powerful ways. Many have shared how God helped them feel better when they were sick, gave them courage when they faced something hard, or made them feel loved when they felt alone.

These stories help us understand that God is always at work and that He cares about each one of us, no matter what we're going through.

What If I Still Have Doubts?

It's perfectly okay to have questions about God. Even grownups wonder about Him sometimes. Having doubts doesn't mean you don't believe. It means you're curious and want to learn more.

Think of questions like stepping stones on a path. Each step you take helps you move closer to God. As you keep asking and exploring, you'll learn more about who He is, and your faith can grow stronger.

You can learn more by reading the Bible, praying, or talking to a parent or pastor. God wants you to ask questions and discover who He really is.

> "Show me your ways, LORD, teach me your paths.
> Guide me in your truth and teach me."
> — Psalm 25:4–5

What to Remember

We can't see God with our eyes, but we can see the clues all around us. We see them in the beauty of creation, our sense of right and wrong, the history of the Bible, and countless other ways. Each of these things points to God, and they're just a few of the ways He shows us who He is. When we put all the clues together, we can be sure God is real, and that He loves us more than we can ever imagine.

TALK ABOUT IT

1. What's one thing in nature that makes you think about God as our Creator?

2. How does your sense of right and wrong help you remember that God is real?

3. God showed Himself through Jesus, but He also gives us clues in the world around us. Why do you think He wants us to notice both?

Chapter 2

How Do We Know Christianity Is True?

There are many religions in the world, but what makes Christianity different? How can we know if it's the true path to God?

In this chapter, we'll explore the evidence and discover why so many people trust Jesus and follow His teachings.

The Unique Story of Jesus

At the very heart of Christianity is Jesus. He wasn't just a regular person. The Bible tells us that He is the Son of God and also God Himself. He is fully God and fully human, and He came to Earth to rescue us.

Jesus did amazing things. He calmed storms, walked on water, healed the sick, and taught with incredible wisdom. But the most important part of His story is what happened at the cross. Jesus died, was buried in a tomb, and came back to life three days later (1 Corinthians 15:3–4). This is called the resurrection, and it shows us that Jesus truly is who He said He is.

Why? Because if Jesus really rose from the dead, it proves He has power over death. That means everything He said about God, life, and how we should live can be trusted. It shows that He truly is the Son of the one true God (John 14:6).

The Bible Is a Trustworthy Guide

The Bible is more than just a book. It's God's Word. God gave His message to people and guided them as they wrote it down (2 Peter 1:21). But how do we know we can trust it?

One powerful reason is that the Bible contains prophecies. A prophecy is when God tells people what will happen before it happens. Long before many events ever took place, God spoke to certain people, called prophets, and they carefully wrote His words down. Years later, those prophecies were fulfilled exactly as God said they would be. This didn't happen just once. It happened many times throughout the Bible.

Some of the most amazing prophecies are about Jesus. They were written hundreds of years before He was born and later came true with incredible detail. There are even some prophecies that point to future events still to come, such as Jesus' return and the final judgment.

Here are a few examples of prophecies that have already come true:

Where Jesus Would Be Born

Hundreds of years before Jesus was born, God told the prophet Micah that the Savior would be born in Bethlehem

(Micah 5:2). And that's exactly where Jesus was born (Matthew 2:1).

How Jesus Would Suffer

The prophet Isaiah wrote that someone would be "pierced" and punished for the sins of others (Isaiah 53:3–5). That was written long before crucifixion was practiced in Israel. Crucifixion was a very painful way of killing people in ancient times, where they were nailed to a wooden cross. Isaiah's words match what happened to Jesus exactly (John 19:34–37).

The Bible also lines up with what we find in archaeology and history. Many cities, rulers, and events mentioned in the Bible have been confirmed by what experts have found.

Along with what we find outside the Bible, the words inside have been carefully kept safe. Over thousands of years, people have copied the Bible with great care. The words we read today are almost identical to the oldest copies ever discovered.

Because of all this evidence, we can trust what the Bible says. It's like when someone makes a promise and keeps it over and over, you learn to trust them. That's what the Bible has done. It's been proven true again and again.

That's why Scripture says:

> "The grass withers and the flowers fall,
> but the word of our God endures forever."
> — Isaiah 40:8

Christianity Transforms Lives

Have you ever seen a caterpillar turn into a butterfly? It's a total change! Christianity has that same kind of power to transform people from the inside out.

Throughout history, people have shared how believing in Jesus gave them peace, purpose, and a fresh start. They talk about feeling completely forgiven from the things they've done wrong, like a heavy burden has been lifted from their hearts. They describe finding joy that replaces deep sadness, and experiencing a love so strong it fills the empty places inside them (2 Corinthians 5:17).

That same change was seen in the lives of Jesus' first followers, right from the very beginning of Christianity. It changed them so powerfully that it shaped how they lived and what they were willing to face.

The Early Church Wouldn't Give Up

After Jesus rose from the dead, His followers began telling everyone what they had seen and heard. They shared that Jesus was alive and that He truly was the Son of God. But believing in Jesus didn't make their lives easier. In many ways, it made them much harder.

Many of Jesus' first followers were warned to stop talking about Him. Some were arrested, beaten, thrown into prison, and even killed for continuing to share the truth (Acts 4:18–20; 5:40–42). Following Jesus cost them their comfort, their safety, and sometimes their lives.

This type of persecution wasn't just recorded in the Bible. Some of the non-Christian writers we learned about in Chapter One documented it as well.

If the disciples had made up the story about Jesus rising from the dead, they could have saved themselves by admitting it wasn't true. But they didn't. They kept telling the same message, even when it led to their suffering. People might tell a lie to get out of trouble, but they don't willingly die for something they know is false. The disciples believed Jesus was alive because they had seen Him with their own eyes (1 Corinthians 15:5–8).

Christianity didn't spread because it was easy or popular. It spread because people were convinced it was true. From the very beginning, followers of Jesus were willing to stand firm in their faith, no matter what the cost.

Christianity's Impact on the World

Jesus taught that every person matters to God, including the poor, the weak, and the forgotten. Because of this, Christians began caring for people others often ignored. From the very beginning, followers of Jesus cared for the sick, helped widows and orphans, and believed that every life had value. They lived this way because Jesus told them to love others the same way that He loved them (John 13:34–35).

These ideas didn't fade away over time. As Christianity grew, they continued to shape the world. Many hospitals, schools, and charities were started by Christians who believed that loving God also meant caring for people in need. Even today, many groups that care for others are built on these same beliefs.

Christianity also shaped how people think about right and wrong. Ideas like forgiveness, mercy, and honesty are woven throughout Jesus' teachings. Over time, these values have influenced laws in many countries, helping to protect people and treat them fairly.

Even in places where people don't follow Jesus, many still believe these values matter. That lasting influence points back to something true and powerful at the heart of Christianity.

What About Other Denominations?

You might wonder, *If Christianity is true, why are there so many different groups of Christians?*

These groups are called denominations. They all believe that Jesus is God's Son and trust the Bible as their guide, though some teachings and traditions may be understood or practiced differently. Some examples include Baptists, Lutherans, and Pentecostals, but there are many others.

When people choose a church to attend, that church may be part of a denomination. What matters most isn't the name of the denomination, but whether the church teaches the truth of the Bible and helps you grow closer to God.

If you do become part of a church that's connected to a denomination, just remember that some traditions come from people, not Scripture, so it's important to check everything against God's Word (Acts 17:11).

What to Remember

The story of Jesus, the reliability of the Bible, the courage of the early church, and the way lives are changed all point to Christianity being true.

God hasn't asked us to believe without any reason. He gave us real evidence, and He continues to show us who He is through His Word, His work in the world, and His love in our hearts.

As you keep asking questions, you'll discover even more ways that God shows us Christianity is the true path to knowing Him.

TALK ABOUT IT

1. What part of Jesus' story shows you that He's more than just a regular person?

2. Why is it important to know that the Bible's prophecies come true?

3. How have you seen God change someone's life, whether in the Bible, in history, or in your own family?

Chapter 3

How Did the Bible Come to Be and Why Are There So Many Versions?

Have you ever wondered how we got the Bible? It's not just any book. It's God's special message to us, filled with incredible stories.

There's Jonah, who was swallowed by a huge fish (Jonah 1–2), Daniel, who was thrown into a den of lions just for praying (Daniel 6), and Jacob, who had a wild wrestling match with an angel (Genesis 32:24–30).

And it's more exciting than any storybook, because these things actually happened. Every part of the Bible helps us understand who God Is and how He wants us to live.

Let's take a journey to discover how this amazing book came to be.

Many Writers, One Story

The Bible isn't one big book written by just one person. It's actually a collection of smaller books, written by more than 40 different people over 1,500 years.

One verse says, "All Scripture is God-breathed" (2 Timothy 3:16). That means the words in the Bible come from God and carry His authority, even though they were written by human hands.

God worked through many different people, guiding each writer by His Spirit. Some wrote about things they experienced, like miracles they saw, lessons they learned, and the way God worked in their lives (2 Peter 1:21). Others wrote poems, prophecies, or letters to churches. Even though they lived in different places and at different times, all their books fit together to tell one unified story about God and His love for us.

Imagine you have a group of friends, and each of you writes a story about a special adventure. Then, you put all the stories together to make one big book. That's kind of like how the Bible was written. It has lots of voices, but God is the author behind them all.

Writing on Special Materials

A long time ago, people didn't have notebooks or computers to write with. They used things like papyrus (a kind of plant paper) and parchment (made from animal skins). They wrote with feather quills or sharpened reeds, and the ink came from things like charcoal and plant juice.

Writing was slow and required great care. Just imagine writing a whole book with a feather! It shows how valuable these words were. People spent a lot of time and effort to make sure they were written accurately and protected for the future.

Passed Down Through Generations

After the books were written, they were carefully copied and shared with others. People treasured these writings as messages from God. Scribes worked hard to copy them exactly, checking their work with responsibility and care.

Sometimes, they compared newer copies to older ones to make sure nothing had changed. Ancient scrolls like the Dead Sea Scrolls help us see how accurate these copies are, even after thousands of years. Jesus once said, "Not the smallest letter, not the least stroke of a pen, will by any means disappear from the Law" (Matthew 5:18). God's Word does not fade away, even as the years go by.

The Old Testament and The New Testament

The Bible has two main parts, and together they tell one big story about God's plan to rescue His people.

The Old Testament is the first part. It tells how God created the world, chose the people of Israel, and made promises to guide and bless them. It includes stories of people like Noah, who built a huge ark and trusted God during a worldwide flood (Genesis 6–9), Moses, who led God's people out of slavery in Egypt (Exodus 1–14), and David, the young shepherd boy who defeated a giant warrior and later became king (1 Samuel 17; 2 Samuel 5–7). It also has the words of prophets who shared messages from God about things He planned to do in the future.

The New Testament is the second part. It tells the story of Jesus, God's Son, who came to Earth to rescue us from sin and bring us close to God again (Luke 2; John 3:16). It also explains how the good news about Jesus spread and how the first Christians built the early church (Acts 1–2). It even gives us a glimpse of what God says is still to come (Revelation 21–22).

Together, the Old and New Testaments reveal God's great love for us from the beginning of time and into eternity.

Putting It All Together

Over many years, wise and faithful followers of God worked together to collect the books that belonged in the Bible. They prayed and asked God to help them recognize the writings that truly came from Him and were already trusted by the early church. Once these books were gathered, they were joined together to form the Bible we know today. Now we have one big, incredible book that tells God's story and teaches us about His love, grace, and wisdom.

What About Bible Versions?

Have you ever noticed that there are different versions of the Bible, like the KJV, NIV, or NLT? That's because the Bible was first written in other languages, mostly Hebrew and Greek. Translators created different versions in everyday languages so people all over the world could understand it.

Some versions use older, more traditional words like "thee" and "thou." Others use simpler words that are easier to understand. But as long as the version is translated faithfully, the message stays the same. God loves us, and He wants to save us.

Great Bible versions for kids and teens include the New International Version (NIV) and the New Living Translation (NLT). They use everyday words, making them easier to read while still staying true to what the Bible means. The King James Version (KJV) is a more traditional option. Its poetic and classic style has been loved for hundreds of years, but some of its older words can be hard to understand.

If you're ever unsure which version is right for you, ask a trusted Christian adult or visit a website like BibleGateway.com to compare how different versions explain the same verses.

But here's something really important to remember. Not all Bible versions are trustworthy. Some versions change or add wording in ways that don't match what the original Bible said. This can lead people to misunderstand what God is trying to teach us. That's why it's best to stick with trustworthy versions, like the ones just mentioned, so you can feel confident about what you're reading.

What to Remember

The Bible is more than just a book. It's the true story of God's love for the world.

It took about 1,500 years and more than 40 writers to complete the Bible, yet every part fits together to share one powerful message. God is real, He loves you, and He wants a relationship with you.

From the very beginning, God made sure His words were written down, protected, and passed on. Today, we can still read those same words in trustworthy Bible versions.

So when you open the Bible, you're not just reading history. You're stepping into God's story. It's a story He invites you to be part of. And the more you read it, the more your faith can grow as you discover just how much God truly cares for you.

TALK ABOUT IT

1. Why do you think it's special that the Bible has many different writers but still tells one story about God's love?

2. How does it help your faith to know that God protected His words over time so we can still read them today?

3. Why is it important to read from Bible versions that stay true to what God really said?

Chapter 4

Can Archaeology Back Up the Bible's Claims?

Have you ever questioned whether the stories in the Bible really happened? It's something many people wonder about.

To find answers, archaeologists act like detectives who dig up clues from the past. And guess what? They've found some pretty cool things that match what the Bible tells us.

These discoveries help us see that the Bible is connected to real places, real people, and real history, which can make our faith even stronger.

Incredible Discoveries That Support the Bible

Here are some things archaeologists have found that help bring this wonderful book to life:

The City of Jericho

Do you remember the story where the walls of Jericho came tumbling down after God told the Israelites to march, shout, and blow their trumpets? Some people thought that story was just a legend.

But archaeological digs at the site of Jericho uncovered collapsed walls, burned buildings, and broken pottery. Some archaeologists believe the whole city was destroyed all at once, matching the story that Joshua 6 describes.

The Split Rock of Horeb

In the wilderness, when the Israelites had no water to drink, God told Moses to strike a rock with his staff, and water came flowing out (Exodus 17:5–6).

Today in the desert of modern-day Jordan stands a giant rock split down the middle. It's about 50 feet tall and shows signs of water erosion at its base. Some people believe this could be the very rock Moses struck. There's no way to know for sure, but the rock's towering height, unique split, and weathered base make it an incredible match for the story described in the Bible.

The House of David

King David is a major figure in the Old Testament. He defeated Goliath (1 Samuel 17), wrote many psalms, and became a great king (2 Samuel 5:3–4). For a long time, some people wondered if David was a real person.

Then in 1993, archaeologists discovered a stone called the Tel Dan Stele, dating back to the 9th century BC, almost 1,000 years before Jesus was born. It was carved in the kingdom of Aram. At that time, Aram was one of Israel's enemies. On the stone, a king brags that he killed the "king of Israel" and a ruler from the "House of David."

His bragging proves that other nations knew about Israel and David's royal family. David had lived long before this, but it shows that his family line was still ruling in Israel. This discovery is strong evidence that David was a real historical king, just like the Bible says.

The Taylor Prism and King Hezekiah

The Bible tells us that when a powerful army attacked Jerusalem, King Hezekiah prayed, and God rescued the city (2 Kings 18–19).

Then in 1830, archaeologists discovered a six-sided clay tablet called the Taylor Prism. It was written by the enemy king of Assyria, who claimed he had attacked many cities but admitted that he couldn't capture Jerusalem. This discovery matches the Bible's account and shows how God protected His people.

The Pool of Siloam

The Bible tells us that Jesus gave sight to a blind man at the Pool of Siloam in Jerusalem (John 9). For a long time, no one knew exactly where that pool was.

But in 2004, workers fixing a sewer line uncovered ancient stone steps buried underground. Archaeologists quickly began digging and uncovered a large pool that dates back to the first century, about 2,000 years ago. Its location, size, and stone-step design point strongly to it being the real Pool of Siloam. Plus, coins and pottery found there confirm it was in use during the time Jesus was alive.

The Stone of Pontius Pilate

Pontius Pilate was a Roman leader called a prefect, similar to a governor. He oversaw Jesus' trial and ordered His crucifixion (Matthew 27:24–26). For a long time, some people wondered if Pilate was real.

Then in 1961, archaeologists found a large stone in the ruins of an ancient Roman city on the coast of Israel. Carved into the stone were the words "Pontius Pilatus, Prefect of Judea." *Pilatus* is the Latin form of *Pilate*. This discovery confirms that Pilate was a real historical leader, exactly as the Bible describes.

Why This Matters

These discoveries remind us that the Bible isn't just a book of stories. It's a true record of God's work in the world.

Finding these places and artifacts helps us trust that the Bible is real and reliable. It's not a book someone made up. It's based in history, and God made sure that His Word would stand the test of time.

Archaeology can strengthen our confidence, but faith is about more than finding proof. God wants us to trust Him because of who He is and what He's done, not just because of what we can see or prove.

The Bible says:

> "Now faith is confidence in what we hope for
> and assurance about what we do not see."
> — Hebrews 11:1

What to Remember

The Bible is connected to real places, real people, and real history.

Archaeology helps show that what the Bible says really happened. These discoveries can make our faith stronger, but our trust in God can go even deeper than that. Even if we never saw a single artifact, we could still believe, because God speaks through His Word, His Spirit, and His love.

The more we explore, the more we see that the Bible truly is God's trustworthy story for us.

TALK ABOUT IT

1. Which discovery from archaeology do you think is the most exciting, and why?

2. How do these discoveries help you see that the Bible is about real people and real places?

3. Why do you think God wants us to trust Him even beyond the things we can see or prove?

Chapter 5

Are Miracles Real?

The Bible is filled with incredible stories that sound almost too wild to be true, like a talking donkey, bread falling from the sky, and people being raised from the dead. These events are called miracles.

But what if these stories are more than just old tales? What if they're real moments where God showed His power in big ways?

In this chapter, we'll explore what miracles are, why they matter, and how they remind us that nothing is impossible for God.

What Is a Miracle?

A miracle is when God steps in and does something amazing that could never happen on its own, something far beyond how science or nature normally work. They're not magic tricks or illusions. Miracles are real acts of God that surprise us and remind us that He is in control.

Here's one way to think about it. If you had a deep cut on your finger, your body would take days or weeks to heal. But if it healed instantly, right before your eyes, that would be a miracle.

Miracles in the Bible

The Bible is packed with amazing miracles.

Here are just a few:

A Donkey Talks

A man named Balaam was going somewhere he shouldn't, so God sent an angel to block his path. Balaam didn't see the angel, but the donkey he was riding on did. The donkey stopped, turned aside, and even lay down, frustrating Balaam. Then miraculously, the donkey spoke! It explained everything and helped Balaam realize that God was trying to get his attention (Numbers 22:21–34).

This story tells us that when we're not listening, God might use surprising ways to speak to us.

Manna from Heaven

When the Israelites were wandering in the desert and had no food, God provided for them by sending manna from the sky. Manna was a bread-like substance that fell to the ground nearly every morning, and the people could gather just enough to eat for each day. It was God's daily reminder that He would take care of them (Exodus 16:4–15).

This miracle shows that God provides for us, even in the hardest times.

Jesus Feeds 5,000 People

A huge crowd gathered to hear Jesus teach, but they didn't have enough food to go around. The disciples wanted to send the people into town to buy food, but Jesus told them to have everyone stay. Then they noticed a boy who had five loaves of bread and two fish. Jesus blessed the food and made it multiply. Over 5,000 people ate until they were full, with plenty of leftovers to spare (Matthew 14:13–21; John 6:9).

This miracle teaches us that no gift is too small for God to use in a big way.

The Red Sea Splits in Two

When the Israelites were trapped between the Red Sea and an army chasing them, God performed an incredible miracle. A strong wind blew all night and pushed the waters of the sea apart. Huge walls of water rose up, towering on each side of a dry path below. The Israelites were able to walk across the sea on dry ground and escape safely (Exodus 14:21–22).

This shows us that God can rescue us, even when things seem impossible.

Jesus Raises the Dead

One of Jesus' friends, Lazarus, had died, and his body was buried in a tomb. When Jesus arrived at the tomb, Lazarus had been dead for four days, and everyone thought there was no hope. But Jesus called him out by name, and to everyone's shock, Lazarus came walking out alive (John 11:38–44).

This miracle shows that Jesus has power over life and death.

Why Miracles Matter

Miracles remind us that God is real and powerful (Psalm 77:14). They help us see that He's still working in the world, and that He cares about what happens to us.

When we read about miracles in the Bible, we see God's strength and kindness. Many of them also show that Jesus truly is God's Son (John 20:30–31).

Whether it's something we read in Scripture or something we experience in our own lives, each miracle helps us understand God's heart. They show us that His heart is full of love, mercy, and healing.

Believing in the Impossible

Sometimes, miracles can be hard to believe, and that's okay. Faith means trusting God, even when we can't see how He's working (Hebrews 11:1).

Think about planting a seed. You don't see what's happening underground, but you can believe something is growing.

Or think about the wind. You can't see it, but you can see what it does. You see trees bend, leaves move, and clouds drift across the sky. You know the wind is real, even though it's invisible.

In the same way, we can trust that God is at work, even when we don't see how. When we believe in the impossible, we make room for God to do amazing things in our lives.

Miracles Today

Miracles didn't stop after they were written about in the Bible. They still happen today. We might not see waters parting, but we do see God at work in other ways.

Some people share stories of healing that they believe came from God, when even doctors couldn't explain how it happened. Others say they were helped at just the right time, like receiving an envelope of money from a stranger when they couldn't afford to buy food.

Even small miracles, like peace during a scary moment, show us that God is still with us. He's showing His love in quiet but powerful ways.

What to Remember

Miracles show us that nothing is too hard for God (Luke 18:27). They remind us that He's always with us, He cares about every detail of our lives, and He's still doing incredible things today.

Whether we notice big miracles or small ones, we can trust that God's power and love never change. He's working for our good, even when we can't see it.

TALK ABOUT IT

1. Which miracle from the Bible stands out to you the most, and why?

2. How do miracles help us see who God is and how much He cares for us?

3. Can you think of a time when God did something in your life that felt like a miracle?

Chapter 6

If God Made Everything, Then Who Made God?

Have you ever looked up at a bright, starry sky and thought, *Wow, God made all of this?* It's amazing to think about. God made the oceans, the mountains, and every person. But that big idea often leads to another big question. *If God made everything, then who made God?*

Asking this question is like trying to find the beginning of everything. We're used to things having a starting point. Toys are made in factories, houses are built by people, and even the Earth had a beginning. So it's normal to wonder about God, who made the universe and everything in it.

God Has No Beginning

To understand the answer, we need to remember that God is unlike anything else. No one created Him. God has always existed. He lives outside of time, which means He has no beginning and no end (Psalm 90:2).

Imagine a number line that goes on forever in both directions. Now picture something even greater than that. Instead of being on the line, it exists outside of it entirely. That's a little like how God is.

When Moses asked God what His name was, God answered, "I AM WHO I AM" (Exodus 3:14). That means God just is. He didn't come from anyone or anything. He exists all on His own.

God Is the First Cause

God didn't come from something else. He is the power behind everything that exists, the source of all life and creation (Genesis 1:1).

If everything has to be made by something else, then there would be no "first thing." There would be no beginning at all, and the universe wouldn't exist. It would be like an endless chain of things being made, and there would be no one to start the chain. But the universe does have a beginning, so there must be a First Cause. God is that First Cause, and He wasn't made by anyone. He simply exists.

Faith in What We Cannot See

We may not fully understand how God can exist without being created. But we can trust Him.

Faith means trusting God even when we can't see everything clearly (Hebrews 11:1). It's like trusting that the sun will rise tomorrow, or that gravity will keep your feet on the ground. And just like the stars stretch farther than we can imagine, God's existence reaches beyond time, space, and everything we know.

We can trust God because He's shown us His love in our hearts, His power in creation, and His promises in the Bible.

What to Remember

The question "Who made God?" helps us think about how special He really is.

God is eternal, with no beginning and no end. He didn't come from something else but is the One who started everything.

Even if we don't understand it all, we can trust that God is real, powerful, and full of love. The God who has always existed made you on purpose and knows you by name. And that's a beautiful thing to remember.

TALK ABOUT IT

1. Why do you think it's hard for us to imagine something that has no beginning or end?

2. How does knowing that God is the First Cause of everything help us trust Him more?

3. What does it mean to you that the God who has always existed is the same God who made you?

Part 2

Becoming Who God Made You to Be

Chapter 7

What Does It Mean to Be a Christian?

Have you ever wondered what it really means to be a Christian? It's more than just a word. It's about making a life-changing decision in your heart.

Let's explore what that decision means and how it shapes the way Christians live every day.

What Is a Christian?

To be a Christian means believing in and following Jesus Christ. It's not just knowing about Him, but trusting that He is the Son of God, the Savior of the world, and the example of how we should live. This belief isn't just a feeling. It's rooted in the teachings of the Bible. Christians believe the Bible is God's message to us, filled with wisdom, love, and hope.

When we believe in Jesus and choose to follow Him, we accept that He willingly died on the cross to take the punishment we deserved for our sins. And three days later, He came back to life. His death and resurrection are the heart of Christianity, showing how much God loves us, how far He would go to save us, and the path He created for us to have eternal life with Him.

Core Beliefs of Christianity

Being a Christian means having some important beliefs that shape how we see the world.

Here are a few of them:

- **One God:** Christians believe in one God who made everything in the universe. He created the heavens, the Earth, and every living thing (Genesis 1:1). This same God also loves us, saves us, and helps us every day. Everything good begins with Him, and everything we need comes from Him.

- **The Trinity:** God is one but He exists in three Persons, who are God the Father (our Creator), God the Son (Jesus, who came to Earth to save us), and God the Holy Spirit (His presence and power living inside of us and helping us) (Matthew 3:16–17).

- **Sin:** Sin isn't just an accident or a mistake. It's when we choose to go against God's commands in our thoughts, words, or actions. These choices are wrong and they create a separation between us and God (Romans 3:23). Sin is like a broken bridge that keeps us apart from Him. No matter how hard we try, we can't fix that bridge on our own.

- **Salvation:** Christians believe that God sent Jesus to Earth to fix that separation. When Jesus died and rose again, He built the bridge back to God. If we believe in Jesus and accept Him as our Savior, our sins are forgiven and we're given the greatest gift of all, the gift of eternal life (Romans 6:23).

- **The Bible:** Christians treasure the Bible as God's special book. It's full of stories and wisdom that help us live in a way that honors Him (Psalm 119:105).

How Christians Live

Being a Christian is more than just saying you believe these things. It's about showing it in the way you live.

Here are some ways Christians live out their faith:

- **Prayer:** Christians talk to God through prayer. It's a time to thank Him, ask for help, and share what's on their hearts. Prayer helps them grow closer to God and reminds them that He's always listening (Philippians 4:6).

- **Bible Study:** Reading the Bible helps Christians learn more about who God is and what He wants for their lives. It teaches them how to live like Jesus and love others the way He does (2 Timothy 2:15).

- **Fellowship:** Spending time with one another at church, in friendships, and in everyday moments helps Christians grow together. They encourage one another, pray for each other, and grow in faith side by side (Hebrews 10:24–25).

- **Service:** Helping others is one way Christians follow Jesus. By giving their time, putting others first, and showing kindness, they share His love with the world (Mark 10:45).

- **Character:** Christians try to live with honesty, patience, and compassion. They want their lives to reflect Jesus' heart and shine His light to others every day (Galatians 5:22–23).

A Life-Changing Decision

The choice to become a Christian is the most important decision you'll ever make. It means saying yes to God's love and asking Jesus to lead your life. When you do, your life changes for the better and becomes filled with hope, purpose, and joy.

If you're ready to make that decision today, here's a simple prayer you can say from your heart:

Dear Jesus,

I know I need You. I believe You are God's Son, who died on the cross for my sins and rose again. Please come into my heart and be my Savior. Please forgive me for the things I've done wrong. Help me make good choices and follow You for the rest of my life. Thank You for loving me and giving me a fresh start.

Amen.

If you prayed that prayer and meant it, you've just made the most important decision of your life. You've chosen to turn your heart toward Jesus and begin a new journey with Him, one you'll never have to walk alone.

What to Remember

Being a Christian means walking with God and letting your faith guide how you live. It's not just about what you believe. It's about living out your faith in real and meaningful ways.

Christianity is a journey that changes you from the inside out. As you grow closer to God, you'll find true peace and purpose. You'll learn to love others the way Jesus does and discover the joy of serving with your whole heart.

The journey won't always be easy, but it brings the greatest reward of living forever in God's presence.

TALK ABOUT IT

1. What does it mean to trust in Jesus and not just know about Him?

2. How can prayer, reading the Bible, or helping others show that you are following Jesus?

3. Why is becoming a Christian such an important decision for your life?

Chapter 8

How Can I Live Like Jesus?

Imagine living each day with the same love, kindness, and courage that Jesus shows. Living like Jesus means more than just knowing about Him. It means choosing to follow His example in how we treat others, how we forgive, and how we serve. When we live like Jesus, our lives reflect His love and bring real change to the world around us.

What Is Jesus Like?

To live like Jesus, we first need to know what He's like. The Bible shows us a clear picture of His heart and how He treats people.

Here are some qualities that make Him our perfect example:

- **He Is Loving:** Jesus cares deeply about others. He shows love to everyone, especially those who are hurting, lonely, or rejected. He loves His friends, strangers, and even His enemies (John 13:34).

- **He Is Forgiving:** Jesus forgives people when they sin and come to Him with a truly sorry heart. He doesn't hold grudges but always gives people the chance to start fresh and live differently (Luke 23:34).

- **He Is Honest:** Jesus always tells the truth and teaches people about God with wisdom and love. He never says things just to please people or win their approval. He speaks with boldness and courage, even when it's hard to hear (Luke 20:21).

- **He Is Courageous:** Jesus stands up for what's right, even when it's difficult. He defends the truth, helps those in need, and follows God's will no matter the cost (Matthew 21:12–13).

- **He Is Humble:** Jesus puts others first. He doesn't go around seeking attention. He chooses to serve rather than be served, living simply and caring for people with compassion (Mark 10:45).

How Can We Live Like Jesus?

Living like Jesus doesn't mean we have to get everything right. It's about growing closer to Him each day and letting His love guide our choices.

Here are some simple ways to live like Jesus:

- **Choose Love:** Treat people with kindness, even when it's hard. Love your friends, your family, and even those who are tough to get along with.

- **Be Quick to Forgive:** Let go of anger and give others the chance to start again. Forgiveness brings peace to your heart and shows people what God's love is like.

- **Tell the Truth:** Be honest in what you say and do. Let your words encourage others and show that you can be trusted.

- **Be Brave for What's Right:** Stand up for what's true and good, even when it's hard or when others disagree. Doing what honors God takes courage.

- **Put Others First:** Look for ways to care for people around you. Share with them, listen to them, and help them whenever you can, in big ways and small ones.

Jesus Is Our Example

You don't have to be perfect to live like Jesus. We all make mistakes, but God's grace helps us keep going.

Living like Jesus is a lifelong journey of becoming more like Him. Every step brings you closer to the person God created you to be (1 Peter 2:21).

What to Remember

Jesus is our example and the One who shows us God's love, a love that is strong, forgiving, and never-ending. As we follow Him, our lives begin to reflect His character and bring light into the world.

Living like Jesus means letting God's love shine through you. It means showing kindness, offering forgiveness, and standing up for what's right. It won't always be easy, but it's the most meaningful way to live.

TALK ABOUT IT

1. Which of Jesus' qualities (loving, forgiving, honest, courageous, or humble) do you want to grow in the most, and why?

2. What's one small choice you could make this week to live more like Jesus?

3. How can showing Jesus' love to others make a difference in the world around you?

Chapter 9

Why Did God Make Me?

Have you ever watched waves crash on the shore, seen birds glide through the sky, or stared up at the moon and felt amazed by it all? Maybe you've wondered, *Why am I here? What's my place in all of this? Why did God make me?*

These are some of the most important questions you can ask, and the answers show just how special you really are.

God Made You Because He Loves You

The most important reason God created you is simply because He loves you. The Bible tells us that "God is love" (1 John 4:8). That means love isn't just something God feels. It's who He is.

He didn't just create the universe filled with stars, or the world filled with trees and animals. He created you because He wanted you to know Him, love Him, and walk through life with Him. It's like a parent longing for a child to love and care for, someone to be close to and guide through life. You are not here by accident. Your story begins with God who made you on purpose, because He delights in you and wants to share a real relationship with you.

You Are Wonderfully Unique

God didn't make anyone else exactly like you. You are one of a kind, with your own personality, talents, and dreams. Just like every snowflake is different, you are a completely unique creation.

The Bible says that God knows everything about you, even the number of hairs on your head (Luke 12:7). Every part of who you are, from your courage to your ideas to your smile, comes from Him so you can share His love in a way that no one else can. He designed you on purpose, and He treasures every detail.

You Have Special Gifts to Share

God has given you special gifts. These might be things you enjoy doing, talents you're good at, or ways you can help others. Maybe you're great at making people laugh or comforting your friends when they're sad. Maybe you love building things, creating art, or coming up with big ideas.

Whatever your gifts are, they're part of God's plan for you. He gave them to you so you could make a difference by bringing His kindness, truth, and love into the lives of others. When you use your gifts to bless others, you become part of the way God is working in the world (1 Peter 4:10).

God Has a Purpose for Everyone

The Bible is filled with stories of people who God chose to do incredible things. He created each person for a reason, and gave them exactly what they needed to carry out His plan.

- **Esther:** She was a young woman who became queen in a foreign land. When her people, the Jews, were in danger of being killed, Esther bravely went to the king, risking her own life to help save them (Esther 4:14–16).

- **Joseph:** He went through many hard times, including being betrayed by his brothers and sold into slavery. But God was with Joseph, guiding him into a position of power in Egypt, where he used his wisdom to save an entire nation from famine (Genesis 45:4–8).

- **Samuel:** He was just a child when he first heard God's voice calling his name. As he grew, Samuel became a faithful prophet who shared God's messages with Israel. God also gave him the important job of anointing the nation's first kings (1 Samuel 3:1–10; 10:1; 16:13).

These stories show us that God can work through anyone, no matter their age or situation. He made you with the same care and love, and He's guiding your life in ways you may not even notice yet.

You Were Made to Walk with God

Just like Esther, Joseph, and Samuel, you are part of God's story too. But more than anything, He wants you to have a close, loving relationship with Him. Before He calls you to do anything big, His greatest desire is for you to know Him and walk with Him each day.

Walking with God means talking to Him in prayer, learning from His Word, and showing His love to others. These aren't chores to earn His approval. They're ways to get to know Him better and let His light shine through your life.

Your worth doesn't come from chasing one big dream or doing something amazing. You are valuable because you're made in God's image (Genesis 1:27), loved by Him, and belong to Him as His child. Living each day with Him is the very reason you were created, so His love can shape you and overflow to the people around you.

What to Remember

God made you with love and care. You are wonderfully unique and filled with purpose (Psalm 139:13–14). Even when you don't know what the future holds, you can trust God to lead you one day at a time.

You were made to know Him, reflect His love, and take part in the story He's writing in the world. As you walk with Him, He will guide your steps and show you more of His plan for your life.

TALK ABOUT IT

1. How does it make you feel to know that God made you on purpose and with love?

2. What's one gift, talent, or quality God has given you that you can use to help others?

3. What's one way you can walk closely with God in your everyday life?

Chapter 10

Does God Have a Plan for My Life?

Thinking about your future can bring up a lot of questions. One of the biggest is, *What does God want me to do with my life?* God doesn't usually give us a step-by-step map, but He does have a wonderful plan for you, and He wants you to discover it.

God's Big Plan for Everyone

First, it's important to understand that God has a general plan for everyone. His plan is revealed throughout the Bible and includes things like loving Him, loving others, and living a life that honors Him (Matthew 22:37–39).

Another part of God's plan is for us to tell other people about Jesus. This is called the Great Commission, and it means inviting people to know Him and experience His love for themselves (Matthew 28:19–20).

This general plan is the starting point for discovering the unique path God has designed just for you.

The Gifts and Talents God Gave You

Part of that unique path involves the gifts and talents God has given you. These are things you're especially good at or love to do. Maybe you're great at drawing, singing, building, solving puzzles, or cheering people up. Those aren't just fun skills. They're clues pointing to how God might use you.

So ask yourself, *What do I enjoy? What am I naturally good at?* Those answers can help you see how God might be calling you to serve.

The Bible says:

> "Each of you should use whatever gift
> you have received to serve others."
> — 1 Peter 4:10

But it's important to remember that God's purpose for your life will never go against His Word. If what you're doing causes you to dishonor Him or live in a way that disagrees with the Bible, you're not on the right path. God's plan always leads to good things that reflect His love and wisdom.

Ask God for Guidance

The best way to discover God's plan for you is by spending time with Him. When you pray, ask God to guide you and give you wisdom (James 1:5). Ask Him to help you see the path He's leading you on.

Then, open your Bible. It's filled with stories and guidance. God speaks through His Word, and sometimes what you read will connect in a special way to your heart, your gifts, or a situation you're going through.

As you walk in obedience, you can trust God to confirm you're on the right path. He may provide encouragement, give you special opportunities, or send you the help and resources you need.

This is just like what God did for Moses when He called him to lead the Israelites (Exodus 4:1–17). It doesn't mean there won't be challenges, but God will guide you through them.

And even if the answers don't come right away, keep seeking. Moses was 80 years old before God revealed his mission, reminding us that God's timing is perfect, even when it feels slow to us. He may be teaching you patience, trust, and faith while you wait so that you're ready for the next step.

Let Others Help You See Clearly

God can use the people around us to guide and encourage us. Talk with your parents, a pastor, or a trusted Christian adult. They may notice strengths or skills in you that you haven't seen yet.

They can also pray for you and encourage you as you grow. Don't be afraid to ask for their thoughts. The Bible tells us that when we listen to advice and accept guidance, we grow wiser over time (Proverbs 19:20).

Trusting God with the Timing

God's plan usually unfolds little by little, and that's okay. You don't need to see the whole path to take the first step, because God knows exactly where He's leading you.

It's like a kid who really wants to drive a car. They might feel ready, but their parents know they still have some growing to do. It wouldn't be safe or wise to hand them the keys too early. In the same way, God sees the full road ahead of you. He knows what you're ready for and what you still need to learn. He will lead you step by step, at the pace that's best for you.

So try new things. Say yes to opportunities that feel exciting, meaningful, or even challenging. Get involved in activities that help others. Each step of faith helps you grow and gives God room to guide you toward what's next.

God's Plan Might Surprise You

As you trust God's timing, you may discover that His plan looks different than what you expected. You might have one idea for your future, while God has something even better in mind. And sometimes, His plan doesn't move in a straight line. It may begin one way and then lead you in a completely new direction.

That isn't something to fear. It's something to welcome. When you stay open to God's leading, He will place you exactly where you're meant to be.

The apostle Paul wrote:

> "We know that in all things
> God works for the good of those who love him,
> who have been called according to his purpose."
> — Romans 8:28

What to Remember

God has a special plan for your life, and He wants you to discover it step by step. His Word shows you how to live, and the gifts and talents He gave you are part of His design.

Even if the path ahead isn't clear, that's perfectly okay. You don't have to figure everything out right now. Just keep walking with Him, and He will lead you where He wants you to go.

TALK ABOUT IT

1. What's one gift or talent God has given you that you enjoy using?

2. How can prayer and reading the Bible help you discover God's plan for your life?

3. Why is it important to trust God, even when you don't know His whole plan yet?

Chapter 11

How Can I Get Closer to God?

Have you ever wanted to have a super-close friend, someone who truly understands you and is always there for you? Getting closer to God is like having that kind of friendship, but even more special and life-changing.

Let's explore how you can build a stronger relationship with Him. It might just be the greatest thing you'll ever experience.

Knowing God Better

Getting closer to God starts with learning more about who He is. It's like going on an adventure to discover something truly amazing. You begin to understand His deep love for you, how much He cares about every part of your life (Psalm 139:1–4), and the wonderful promises He gives us in the Bible.

You also learn about His eternal plans for you, plans filled with love, purpose, and the hope of Heaven. Having a close relationship with God is like finding a hidden treasure, worth more than anything money can buy.

Ways to Grow Closer to God

Growing closer to God is a lot like tending a garden. It doesn't happen all at once, but with patience and care, it begins to grow.

Here are some ways to help your relationship with God blossom:

Spend Time in Nature

Being outside in God's creation can help you feel His presence. Whether you're walking, sitting, or just looking around, notice the beauty He designed. Think about the softness of grass, the shape of a pinecone, or the sound of birds singing. Use those quiet moments to talk to God or simply thank Him for His wonderful work.

Read the Bible

The Bible helps you understand who God is and how much He loves you (2 Timothy 3:16–17). It's full of stories, promises, and wisdom for your life. You can start small, maybe just one verse a day, and take time to think about what it means. If something is confusing, ask a parent or a trusted Christian adult to explain it. A children's Bible can also be helpful by sharing stories in simpler ways that are easy to follow.

Pray

Talking to God each day helps build your relationship with Him. Prayer is simply sharing your thoughts, worries, hopes, and thankfulness with the One who made you. You can pray out loud or silently, while sitting, walking, or even lying in bed. What matters most is that it's honest and comes from your heart.

Worship and Praise

Worship helps your heart grow closer to God. You can worship by singing songs, writing prayers or poems, or creating art that expresses your love for Him. Worship is a way of saying, "God, You are amazing, and I love You." You can praise Him anytime, whether you're at church, at home, or anywhere else.

Serve Others

Another way to grow closer to God is by showing His love to others. Jesus taught us to serve with kindness and compassion (Mark 10:45). When you help a friend, comfort someone who's sad, or give to someone in need, you're putting God's love into action and drawing closer to Him at the same time.

Peace Over Worry

One of the greatest gifts of knowing God is the peace He gives to your heart. When you feel worried or overwhelmed, being close to Him helps calm those feelings. His presence reminds you that you're not alone and that He is in control, even when life feels confusing (Joshua 1:9).

The more you get to know God, the more you'll learn to let go of fear and trust that He's taking care of you. His love can bring you comfort, strength, and a deep sense of peace that nothing else can give.

The Bible says:

> "Cast all your anxiety on him
> because he cares for you."
> — 1 Peter 5:7

Whatever's weighing on your heart, you can give it to God and rest in the peace He provides.

Seeing the World Differently

When you're close to God, you begin to experience the world in a new way. It's like putting on special glasses that help you notice things you didn't see before. You might see more of the beauty around you, like acts of kindness, little blessings, and signs of how God is working in your life.

As your faith grows, you begin to understand that everything has a purpose and that God is always with you, guiding you through every step of your life (Romans 8:28). You start to view the world with hope and direction, knowing that you can fully trust God's plan.

What to Remember

Getting closer to God is the best decision you could ever make. It can bring you joy, peace, and a love that never fades.

A strong relationship with Him usually doesn't happen all at once, but grows little by little as you spend time with Him and learn to trust Him more. Sometimes you may feel very close to God, and other times you may feel further away, and that's okay. What matters most is that you keep turning to Him.

No matter where you are on your journey, God will always meet you right where you are.

TALK ABOUT IT

1. Which way of getting closer to God (reading the Bible, praying, worshiping, serving, or spending time in nature) sounds most meaningful to you right now?

2. How can knowing God better help you feel at peace when you're worried or afraid?

3. What's one small step you can take this week to grow closer to God?

Chapter 12

Why Do We Worship God?

Think about the last time you clapped or cheered for someone. Maybe it was at a concert, a sports game, or when a friend did something really cool. We celebrate people all the time, like musicians, athletes, and even our friends and family. But what about God? Have you ever thought about celebrating Him?

Worship is how we show God how much we love and appreciate Him. But it goes even deeper than that. Worship helps us connect with God, remind ourselves of His goodness, and grow in our faith.

Let's explore why worship really matters.

Worship Is About Who God Is

Think about all the amazing things God has done. He created the entire universe, from the swirling galaxies in outer space to the waterfalls and wildflowers here on Earth. But He didn't stop there. God also gives us what we need each day, like food to eat, a place to rest, and people who care for us.

God isn't just powerful. He's loving, kind, and faithful (Exodus 34:6). He's not a grumpy king who demands praise just because He can. He's a Father who loves us and wants us to know Him. Worship is our way of saying, "God, You are awesome, and I'm so grateful for You!"

Worship Is About Thanking God

Has anyone ever done something really kind for you, and you couldn't wait to say thank you? Maybe your parents cooked your favorite meal, or a friend cheered you up when you were sad.

God gives us so many good things too, like love that surrounds us, friends who make us laugh, and sunsets that take our breath away. Worship is one way we say, "Thank You, God, for everything You've done!"

James 1:17 tells us that every good and perfect gift comes from God. Worship helps us remember that and thank Him for it.

Worship Is About Showing Our Love

When you really love someone, you want to be close to them. You talk to them, listen to them, and show them you care. Worship is like giving God a big hug from your heart.

It's a way of saying, "God, I love You and I'm so glad You're in my life." Worship reminds us that our relationship with God isn't just about rules. It's about love, peace, and closeness with Him.

Different Ways to Worship

Worship comes in many forms, not just one. There are lots of ways to show God your love and honor Him in everyday life.

Here are a few examples:

Singing

Singing worship songs is a beautiful way to praise God. When we lift our voices and raise our hands, we celebrate who He is, and our hearts fill with thankfulness for all He has done (Psalm 63:4).

The Bible tells us:

> "Worship the LORD with gladness;
> come before him with joyful songs."
> — Psalm 100:2

Prayer

Prayer is a meaningful way to connect with God and worship Him. You can talk to Him anytime, whether you're happy, sad, thankful, or even if you need help with something. God loves hearing your voice, and every prayer brings you closer to Him.

Obedience

Worship isn't just about the words we speak. It's also shown through the way we live. When we choose to follow God's rules, we show our trust and love for Him. Every good choice we make is a way of honoring God with our lives.

Serving Others

Serving others is a powerful way to worship God through what you do. Whether you help someone in need, comfort a friend, or share a word of encouragement, your actions shine God's light into the lives of others. Jesus said that when we serve others, it's like we're serving Him (Matthew 25:40).

Reverence

Reverence is a deep respect and awe for who God is. Some people bow or close their eyes to focus on Him during worship. The Bible says that one day every knee will bow before God (Philippians 2:10). Bowing now can be our way of saying, "God, I worship You as my King."

Worship Isn't Just for Church

Some people think worship only happens on Sundays at church, but that's not true. Worship can happen anywhere, anytime. You can worship when you pray before bed, when you notice the beauty of creation, or when you encourage a friend.

Even something as simple as saying, "Thank You, God," is worship. It's not about being in a special place. It's about having a heart that honors God wherever you are (John 4:24).

What to Remember

Worship is more than just singing songs. It's how we live each day to thank God for His love. It's about respecting who He is, staying close to Him, and showing how much He means to us.

You can worship by singing, praying, helping others, or simply offering your thanks to God. Worship might look different for each person, and that's okay. What matters most is that it's real and comes from your heart. Worship isn't just something we do. It's a way of life.

TALK ABOUT IT

1. What's one thing about who God is that makes you want to worship Him?

2. What are some ways you like to show God your love and thank Him for everything He's done?

3. How can you worship God outside of church in your everyday life?

Chapter 13

What Does It Mean to Trust God?

Imagine you're standing at the edge of a really high diving board. Your heart is pounding, and the pool looks very far below. You know the water will catch you, but taking that first step still feels scary.

Trusting God is kind of like that. It means believing He's there for you, even when you don't know how everything will turn out. It's knowing that He loves you, has a plan for your life, and will never let you down.

Trusting God Means Believing He's Good

The Bible tells us that God is good all the time, not just when life feels easy, but also when things feel confusing or hard (Psalm 100:5). Even when we don't understand what's happening, we know that God is working for our good (Romans 8:28).

Think about your parents or an adult who cares about you. Sometimes they make choices that don't make sense to you, like not letting you watch a certain movie or saying no when you want to go somewhere. You may not always understand their choices, but you trust them because you believe they're good and care about your well-being.

God is like a loving parent, only so much better. He can see the whole story of your life when you can only see a small part. When you choose to believe that God is good, it becomes easier to trust Him.

Trusting God Means Relying on Him

Trusting God isn't just believing certain things about Him. It's also turning to Him when life gets tough. When you're scared, confused, or facing a problem you don't know how to solve, trusting God means going to Him first.

Think about a time when you really depended on someone. Maybe a friend stayed with you when you felt nervous at school, or a parent helped you figure out what to do when you felt stuck. In moments like that, you weren't just believing they cared. You were relying on them to help you.

God wants you to rely on Him in the same way, but even more. He's always ready to listen, guide you, and give you strength when you need it most. You can turn to Him with your questions, your worries, and even the choices you need to make (Philippians 4:6–7).

People in the Bible Who Trusted God

The Bible is filled with stories of people who faced big challenges and chose to trust God anyway. Their lives help us see what real faith looks like.

Noah

Noah trusted God when God told him to build an ark because a huge flood was coming that would cover the entire Earth. Noah lived in a dry place, and the idea of a flood seemed impossible. People probably laughed at him and thought he had lost his mind. But Noah believed God and followed His instructions.

Noah worked hard, building the ark exactly the way God told him to. When the flood came, Noah, his family, and many animals were safe inside. Because Noah trusted God, life was able to continue after the storm (Genesis 6–9).

Abraham

When God told Abraham to leave his home and move to a new land, he didn't know where he was going, but he went anyway. God promised that Abraham's family would grow to become a great nation, and through him, all people on Earth would be blessed.

Even though it meant walking into the unknown, Abraham believed what God said and obeyed. Over time, God led Abraham to the land He had chosen, and kept every word of His promise (Genesis 12:1–5; 15:1–6).

David

David was just a young shepherd when he stepped forward to fight Goliath, a giant warrior who had frightened everyone else. While others ran away, David believed that God would give him the strength to win.

He didn't wear armor or carry a sword. Instead, he picked up five smooth stones and walked into battle with only a slingshot and strong faith. With one stone and God's power, he defeated Goliath. David's courage shows us that no problem is too big when we trust God (1 Samuel 17:40–50).

How Can You Learn to Trust God?

Noah, Abraham, and David each had a choice. They could rely on themselves, or they could trust God, and they chose to trust Him. They didn't always know what would happen next, but they believed God would guide, protect, and take care of them. And He did. As you get to know God better, you can learn to trust Him more too.

Here are some ways you can do that:

- **Learn About Him:** The more you read the Bible, the more you'll discover how faithful and loving God really is. The better you know Him, the easier it becomes to trust Him.

- **Talk to Him:** Prayer is how you build a relationship with God, just like talking to a friend. The more you pray, the more you'll grow to rely on His love and guidance.

- **Obey Him:** Trusting God means following His ways, even when it's hard. When you obey Him, you're showing that you trust His wisdom more than your own.

- **Remember His Faithfulness:** Has God ever helped you before? Did He answer a prayer or give you peace when you were worried? Remembering what He's already done helps you trust Him more in the future.

What to Remember

Trusting God is one of the most important choices you can make in your walk of faith. It means believing in His love, depending on His help, and following His plan. It's not always easy, but it's always worth it.

Just like jumping off a high diving board, the first step might feel scary. But once you take that leap, you'll realize God was there to catch you all along.

TALK ABOUT IT

1. What's one situation in your life right now where it feels hard to trust God?

2. How does the story of Noah, Abraham, or David encourage you to rely on God when things are uncertain?

3. What's one way you can show trust in God this week?

Chapter 14

Why Do Christians Get Baptized?

Think about how we use water every day. It cleans our bodies, quenches our thirst, and helps living things grow. Water has the power to wash away dirt and make things look new. But in baptism, water becomes something even more meaningful. It shows how God has washed away our past through Jesus and given us a brand-new start (2 Corinthians 5:17).

You may have seen someone get baptized at church. A person steps into a small pool, is gently lowered under the water, and then rises up again, like a seed bursting to life.

To understand this powerful picture, let's dive deeper into what baptism is all about.

A Picture of New Life

Baptism isn't just a tradition. It's a way of showing the world the decision you've made in your heart. Baptism is about turning your back on your old life and embracing the new life that Jesus offers.

When someone is baptized, they're gently lowered under water and then brought back up. These are important movements:

- Going under the water shows they're turning away from their old life, leaving behind sin and selfishness.

- Coming up out of the water shows they've been made new, cleansed, forgiven, and ready to follow Jesus.

It's a way of saying, "My life is different now because of Jesus." It also reminds us of what Jesus did for us. He died, was buried, and rose again. Baptism reflects that journey, showing death to the old life and rising into a new life with Him.

Responding to Jesus

Following Jesus means trusting Him and choosing to live His way instead of your own. This includes repentance, which means turning away from sin and turning to God for forgiveness.

It also means responding to His call to be baptized. Remember, baptism doesn't save you. Only faith in Jesus can do that. But baptism is a way to show, on the outside, what has already happened inside your heart. It's a public step that shows your love for Jesus and a desire to follow Him.

The Bible says:

> "Repent and be baptized, every one of you,
> in the name of Jesus Christ for the forgiveness of your sins."
> — Acts 2:38

This shows that repentance and baptism go together as a response to faith. Repentance shows a heart that is changing on the inside, and baptism shows that same change on the outside. Baptism doesn't give you a new life with God, but it points to the new life He's already given you.

Jesus Was Baptized Too

Jesus was baptized in the Jordan River (Matthew 3:13–16). After He came up from the water, the heavens opened, and the Holy Spirit came down like a dove. The Holy Spirit is God's Spirit, who lives inside everyone who trusts in Jesus.

Then God the Father said:

> "This is my Son, whom I love;
> with him I am well pleased."
> — Matthew 3:17

Even though Jesus never sinned, He chose to be baptized. He didn't need to be cleansed, but He wanted to set an example for us. Jesus showed us that baptism is something special. If He stepped into the water to honor God, we can too.

Where and How Can Baptism Happen?

Baptism doesn't have to take place in a church building or in front of a large crowd. It can happen anywhere there's water. The location and type of water don't matter, only the heart of the person being baptized (Acts 8:36–38).

Many people are baptized during church services, while others are baptized in lakes, rivers, swimming pools, or oceans. Some are baptized at summer camp or during a quiet moment with close family and friends. Others, like people in prison, have been baptized in barrels, tubs, or wherever water was available.

Baptism isn't about how perfect or fancy the setting is. The important thing is the faith behind the moment.

Who Can Baptize Someone?

The Bible doesn't give strict rules about who is allowed to baptize someone. But we do see examples in Scripture that show how both the apostles and ordinary followers of Jesus baptized others. The apostles were a special group of men chosen by Jesus to help start the church and lead others in spreading the Gospel.

When Saul (later called Paul) first believed in Jesus, a man named Ananias baptized him (Acts 9:10–18). Ananias wasn't one of the apostles. He was simply a follower of Jesus. Another example is Philip, who baptized a man from Ethiopia after telling him about Jesus (Acts 8:36–38). Philip wasn't an apostle either. He was a faithful believer who shared the Gospel as he traveled.

Before Jesus returned to Heaven, He gave His apostles this command:

"Therefore go and make disciples of all nations,
baptizing them in the name of the Father
and of the Son and of the Holy Spirit,
and teaching them to obey everything
I have commanded you."
— Matthew 28:19–20

Jesus told the apostles to make new disciples and teach them to obey the same commands He gave them. That's why this mission continues today. It shows that every follower of Jesus can have a role in helping others grow in faith, and sometimes that might include baptism.

At the same time, many baptisms in the New Testament did happen through church leaders like the apostles (Acts 10:46–48; 1 Corinthians 1:13–16). Baptism was often a joyful event with the whole church family watching and celebrating together. That's why some churches today require baptisms to happen under the guidance of a pastor or elder. This helps make sure everything is done in line with Scripture and gives the church family a chance to celebrate and support the new believer.

Because Scripture shows flexibility, Christians today sometimes understand and practice baptism a little differently. If you're thinking about baptism, it's a good idea to talk with your pastor and parents first. They can pray with you, make sure you understand what baptism means, and help you celebrate this exciting step of faith.

What If I Was Baptized as a Baby?

Some churches baptize babies as a way of dedicating them to God. It's a special tradition that shows your family wanted you to grow up knowing Jesus. In the Bible, though, baptism always came after someone turned away from their sin, believed in Jesus, and chose to follow Him (Acts 2:41; Acts 8:12, 36–38).

Because of this, some Christians encourage people who were baptized as babies to be baptized later, once they make their own decision to trust Jesus. Others see infant baptism as perfectly fine and don't think it needs to be done again. Since churches differ, it's a good idea to talk with your pastor about how your church approaches this.

But no matter when you're baptized, God sees your heart. What matters most is your personal faith in Jesus and your desire to follow Him.

What to Remember

Baptism is a beautiful step in the Christian journey. It's not just about getting wet. Baptism shows the world that you've chosen to follow Jesus. It's an outward sign of an inward change.

Whether you're baptized at church, in a lake, or with just a few family members, what matters most is your decision to follow Jesus. Baptism doesn't change who you are. It simply shows that you are God's child and want to live a life that honors Him.

Once you've taken that step, don't forget about it. Let it remind you that you've been made new, you belong to God, and that His love is always with you. No matter where life takes you, your baptism can be a moment you look back on with confidence. It marks the day you stood before others and boldly declared, "My heart belongs to Jesus, and I will follow Him for the rest of my life."

TALK ABOUT IT

1. Why do you think baptism is such a powerful way to show that your life belongs to Jesus?

2. How does baptism remind us of what Jesus did when He died and rose again?

3. If you have already been baptized, what does that moment mean to you now? If you have not, what questions do you still have about baptism?

Part 3

Understanding God's Love and Guidance

Chapter 15

Why Can't I Hear God Speaking to Me?

Have you ever wondered why it seems like some people can hear God, but you can't? That's a question many people ask, and it's a good one to talk about. The truth is, God really does communicate with us. You probably won't hear Him speak out loud, but that doesn't mean He isn't speaking to your heart.

Jesus said:

> "My sheep listen to my voice;
> I know them, and they follow me."
> — John 10:27

That means the more we grow in our relationship with Him, the easier it becomes to recognize His voice in our lives.

Let's look at some of the ways God reaches out to us and how you can learn to hear Him more clearly.

How God Communicates

God can communicate with us in many different ways, and it's rarely through a booming voice from the sky. Instead, He uses gentle and loving ways to guide us, encourage us, and remind us of His presence.

Here are some ways He makes His voice known:

Through the Bible

The Bible is God's written Word, and it's the clearest way He speaks to us. When you read the Bible, you're hearing directly from Him. Sometimes a verse will bring you peace, give you direction, or even answer a prayer. The more time you spend in Scripture, the more clearly you'll hear His voice in your heart (2 Timothy 3:16–17).

Through Nature

Creation reflects the greatness of its Creator. A playful breeze, the sound of birds singing, or the warmth of the sun can carry a message of peace or comfort from Him. Nature quiets our hearts and opens our minds to hear Him in ways we might not expect (Psalm 19:1–2; Romans 1:20).

Through Prayer

Prayer isn't just about talking to God. It's also about listening. As you pray, He may remind you of a Bible verse, give you peace during a hard moment, or nudge you to trust Him more. Even if you don't hear back from Him right away, your time with God is never wasted (Philippians 4:6–7).

Through Your Heart

God sometimes gives gentle nudges in your thoughts or feelings. Maybe you sense that you should help someone, or feel peace while making a hard decision. These nudges can be God guiding you to do what's right (Philippians 2:13).

Through What Happens Around You

Sometimes God guides us through the things that happen in our lives. For example, if you were planning to do something and it suddenly doesn't work out, that might be God gently steering you in a different direction. He can use changes, surprises, and even disappointments to help you grow and follow His plan (Proverbs 16:9).

Through Other People

God often uses people to encourage or teach us. A parent, friend, teacher, or pastor may say something that lines up perfectly with what you need to hear. It might feel like they knew exactly what you were going through, but it's really God using their words to guide you (Proverbs 27:17).

Through Singing Worship Songs

When we sing worship songs to God, He can touch our hearts in powerful ways. He may use these moments to remind you that He loves you, calm your worries, fill you with peace, or strengthen your faith. Many songs even use Bible verses in their lyrics, which helps God's Word sink even deeper into your heart (Colossians 3:16).

Why You Might Not Be Recognizing God's Voice

Sometimes, we don't hear God because we're not sure what to listen for.

Here are some reasons why:

You're Expecting a Loud Voice

God almost never speaks out loud. You might be waiting for something dramatic, but His voice is usually quiet and gentle. Instead of expecting something loud, listen for a calm feeling in your heart, a kind thought that pops into your mind, or a small nudge to do what's right (1 Kings 19:12).

You're Not Spending Time with Him

Like any friendship, you need to spend time with God to get to know Him better. If you want to hear from Him, spend time reading the Bible, praying, and worshiping Him. The more time you spend with God, the more clearly you'll recognize His voice (Revelation 3:20).

You're Distracted

It's hard to hear God when life is loud and busy. Try turning off the TV, putting away distractions like toys or devices, and finding a quiet place where you can focus on Him. It's easier to notice God's voice when you are still (Psalm 46:10).

You're Not Sure What to Listen For

God's voice can sound a lot like a wise thought or a loving feeling. It might be hard to tell at first if it's from Him or just from your own mind. As you grow closer to God and learn more about His heart, it becomes easier to recognize His voice in your own thoughts (John 14:26).

You Haven't Asked Him

Have you asked God to communicate with you? Try it! Ask Him to lead you in a way you can understand, maybe through a verse in the Bible, a reminder in your heart, or an encouraging word from someone else. It might not happen right away, but when the time is right, He will make Himself known (Matthew 7:7).

What to Remember

Hearing God's voice takes time and patience. Don't feel discouraged if it doesn't happen right away. Keep spending time with Him, reading the Bible, praying, worshiping, and being still. God loves you and wants you to hear Him. He's always speaking through His Word and guiding believers through His Spirit (Romans 8:14).

It's also important to know that God's guidance will always agree with what the Bible teaches and lead you toward love and goodness. That means not every thought or feeling you have comes from God. As your faith grows, it will become easier to tell the difference between the two and recognize God's gentle guidance throughout your life.

TALK ABOUT IT

1. What's one way you think God might try to get your attention?

2. What are some distractions that might keep you from hearing God's voice, and how could you make more space to listen for Him?

3. How does it make you feel to know that whenever you read the Bible, God is speaking to you through His Word?

Chapter 16

Why Doesn't God Always Answer My Prayers?

Have you ever prayed for something really important, and it felt like God didn't hear you or didn't care? It can be confusing and even frustrating when it seems like nothing is happening. But the truth is, God always hears your prayers, even if the answer isn't what you expected or doesn't happen when you hoped it would.

Let's explore why it may seem God isn't answering you, and how to understand His loving response.

Understanding God's Timing

One of the most important things to remember is that God's timing is perfect. He sees the big picture of your life and knows what's best for you, even when you don't understand why. Sometimes you ask for something you think will bring you happiness in the moment, but God sees how it could affect you in the future.

> "There is a time for everything,
> and a season for every activity under the heavens."
> — Ecclesiastes 3:1

Imagine a gardener planting seeds. Some grow quickly, while others take a long time. The gardener doesn't rush them. He knows exactly when each one will bloom. God is a lot like that gardener. With patience and care, He's always at work in your life, helping you grow and blossom at just the right time.

Different Kinds of Answers

God's answers don't always look the way we expect. Sometimes He says "yes," other times He says "no" and sometimes He says "not yet."

A "no" can feel disappointing, but it's often God protecting us from something harmful or teaching us a valuable lesson.

For example, if you prayed to win a race but didn't win, maybe God is helping you grow in sportsmanship, learn not to give up, or to try again when things don't go your way.

A "not yet" might mean God is preparing something even better than what you asked for. Think of His plan for your life like a puzzle. God is putting all the pieces together, and when the time is right, you'll see the beautiful picture He's been creating.

Sometimes, God answers by giving you what you need instead of what you asked for. He might not take the problem away, but He may send a friend to cheer you up or give you strength to face a tough day. These are answers too, even if they look different from what you wanted.

Scripture tells us:

> "For my thoughts are not your thoughts,
> neither are your ways my ways," declares the LORD.
> "As the heavens are higher than the earth,
> so are my ways higher than your ways
> and my thoughts than your thoughts."
> — Isaiah 55:8–9

God Is Working in Ways We Can't Always See

There's a story in the book of Daniel that shows something happening behind the scenes. Many Christians understand this story as showing us that spiritual battles can be happening in the world, even when we aren't aware of them.

Daniel had been given a vision that he didn't understand, and it troubled him. He prayed and fasted, asking God to help him understand what the vision meant. God sent an angel with a message right away. But the angel was delayed for 21 days because a demon tried to stop him from delivering it. After a powerful angel named Michael came to help, the message finally got through (Daniel 10; 12:1).

This teaches us that God hears us as soon as we pray. But as the story shows, there may be more happening than what we can see. While we don't always know why answers take time, we can trust that God is always at work.

The Importance of Prayer

Even when it feels like God isn't answering, prayer is still powerful. It's more than just asking for things. It's one of the ways you stay close to God, like talking to your best friend. You don't only talk when you need something, but because you care about each other and want to stay connected.

The Bible says it simply:

> "Pray continually."
> — 1 Thessalonians 5:17

When you pray, you're sharing your joys, fears, and dreams with God. You're spending time with Him and building a real relationship. The more you talk to Him, the more you'll trust Him and understand His heart.

Prayer also helps your heart begin to want what God wants. And when His answer to your prayer is different from what you hoped for, you can still talk to Him about it. Ask Him for peace, strength, and understanding as you learn to trust His plan.

The apostle Paul wrote:

> "Do not be anxious about anything,
> but in every situation, by prayer and petition,
> with thanksgiving, present your requests to God."
> — Philippians 4:6

Keep a Prayer Journal

It can be easy to forget how God has answered your prayers, especially when you're still waiting for something. That's why keeping a prayer journal can be really helpful.

A prayer journal is a notebook where you write down what you're praying for and what you're trusting God to do. Later, you can look back and see how He's answered each prayer, whether in a big, obvious way or a small, quiet one.

Reviewing these moments will show you that God is always faithful, even when the answer takes time.

What to Remember

God always hears your prayers, even when the answers don't come the way you expect. Trust His perfect timing. He sees your whole life from beginning to end and is always leading you with love and wisdom. Even when you can't see what He's doing, you can still trust His heart.

Talk to God as much as you can, like when you wake up, before bed, and in simple moments all day long. Tell Him whatever's on your mind, because prayer doesn't have to be long or fancy. What matters most is being honest.

You can also use a journal to track your prayers and write down how God answers them. Over time, you'll start to notice how faithful He is, even in small ways.

As you keep walking with God, you'll see that He's been guiding you all along. So if you ever wonder why a prayer hasn't been answered yet, remember that God hears what you want, knows what you need, and is always working for your good.

TALK ABOUT IT

1. Can you think of a time when God answered a prayer in a way you didn't expect? How did it make you feel?

2. Why do you think God sometimes says "no" or "not yet" instead of "yes"?

3. How could keeping a prayer journal help you see how God is working in your life?

Chapter 17

Does God Care About My Feelings?

Imagine you're having a really bad day. Maybe you didn't do well on a test, your best friend was mean to you, or you just feel sad for no reason at all. When everything feels crummy, you might wonder, *Does God even notice? Does He care how I feel?*

Of course He does! God totally cares about your feelings. He sees the deepest corners of your heart and wants you to bring each of those feelings to Him.

God Made Your Heart to Feel

God didn't make you like a rock that can't feel anything. He gave you a heart that's full of emotions: happy, sad, excited, scared, and lots of others too. He made you this way because feelings are important. They help you understand yourself and the world around you. God loves every part of you, including your feelings.

God Understands Your Feelings

Sometimes, when you're feeling down, people might say things like, "Just get over it." But God never says that. He understands exactly what you're going through.

The Bible says:

> "He heals the brokenhearted
> and binds up their wounds."
> — Psalm 147:3

That means whenever you're sad or hurt, God is right there with you. He can lift your heavy heart like a loving parent giving you a warm hug. Even if you don't feel Him near, you can trust that He's always with you, gently carrying you through.

Talk to God About Your Feelings

You can talk to God anytime, about anything. You don't need special words or a special place. Just tell Him what's on your heart. Whether you're bursting with excitement or weighed down by frustrations, God wants to hear about it. He cares about you and is always listening.

God Is with You in Every Feeling

No matter how you're feeling, God sees it and wants to help. He knows what you're going through, and the Bible has plenty of verses to guide and encourage you.

Here are some ways God can help when your feelings feel too big to handle:

When You're Feeling Worried

God doesn't want you to carry heavy worries by yourself. You can hand them over to Him, and He will help you through.

"So do not fear, for I am with you;
do not be dismayed, for I am your God.
I will strengthen you and help you;
I will uphold you with my righteous right hand."
— Isaiah 41:10

When You're Feeling Scared

God is near, even in the scariest moments. Call out to Him, and His peace can help calm your heart.

> "Even though I walk through the darkest valley,
> I will fear no evil, for you are with me."
> — Psalm 23:4

When You're Feeling Angry

It's okay to tell God when you're angry. He understands. Ask Him to help you settle your heart, show kindness, and forgive others, even when you're upset.

> "Be kind and compassionate to one another,
> forgiving each other,
> just as in Christ God forgave you."
> — Ephesians 4:32

When You're Feeling Lonely

You are never truly alone. God is always with you, even when it feels like no one else is.

> "Never will I leave you;
> never will I forsake you."
> — Hebrews 13:5

When You're Feeling Sad

God cares when sadness weighs you down. You can turn to Him for comfort, and He will be your strength.

"The Lord is close to the brokenhearted
and saves those who are crushed in spirit."
— Psalm 34:18

When You're Feeling Discouraged

Sometimes it feels like nothing is going right, no matter how hard you try. When you feel like giving up, God can remind you that He's with you and will help you keep going.

"Let us not become weary in doing good,
for at the proper time we will reap a harvest
if we do not give up."
— Galatians 6:9

What to Remember

Your feelings matter to God. He made you with emotions and understands every one of them, whether you feel happy, sad, angry, or anything else in between. When you bring those feelings to Him, He won't ignore you or push you away. He listens and can fill your heart with peace.

So the next time you feel something big, remember that God is right there with you, ready to comfort you, guide you, and love you through it all.

TALK ABOUT IT

1. Which feeling is hardest for you to talk about with other people, and how could you share that feeling with God instead?

2. When you're having a bad day, what's one Bible verse from this chapter that could help you remember God's love?

3. How does it make you feel to know that God is always with you, no matter what emotions you're going through?

Chapter 18

How Do I Know God Loves Me When I Don't Feel It?

Sometimes you might feel God's love really strongly, like He's right there with you. Other times, His love may feel quiet or hard to find. Or maybe you've never felt His love before. When God feels distant, you might wonder, *Does He even love me?*

Even if you don't feel it, God's love is always there. He might be showing it in gentle ways that you haven't noticed yet.

This chapter will help you learn how to recognize His love and trust that it's real.

God's Love Is a Promise

The Bible is full of beautiful promises, like God saying He's with you when you're scared (Psalm 23:4) and that He'll never leave you (Deuteronomy 31:6). These promises are reminders of how much He truly cares. And God's words are something you can always count on, no matter how you feel.

God Showed Us His Love

The biggest proof of God's love is what He did for us.

The Bible tells us:

> "For God so loved the world
> that He gave His one and only Son,
> that whoever believes in Him shall not perish
> but have eternal life."
> — John 3:16

God sent Jesus to Earth as a sacrifice to save us from our sins. That wasn't just a kind thought. It was a real action that showed how much He loves us. His choice to send Jesus is the strongest proof that His love is real, powerful, and will never change.

Why We Might Not Feel God's Love

Life can get really noisy and distracting sometimes. School, friends, worries, and responsibilities can crowd your thoughts, making it hard to hear God's quiet voice. It's like trying to hear a whisper in a loud room.

And sometimes, your feelings can be confusing. The Bible says our hearts don't always lead us in the right direction (Jeremiah 17:9). So even if you don't feel God's love, that doesn't mean it isn't there. His love never changes, even when your emotions do.

Everyday Ways to Feel God's Love

God wants you to know and feel His love every day.

Here are some ways you can notice His love all around you:

Through the Bible

The Bible is God's special message to you. When you read it, you're hearing directly from Him (2 Timothy 3:16). It's full of stories showing how God loves His people, even in hard times. The more you read, you'll see that God's love isn't just a feeling. It's something you can depend on. It's like He's saying, "I'm with you, and you're safe with Me."

Through Prayer

Prayer is how you talk to God, trusting that He's listening, even if you can't see or hear Him. It's not about saying the perfect words, but about being honest with your struggles, your questions, and your heart. The more you share with God, the more you'll notice His love guiding you. Prayer helps you trust Him more and grow closer to Him (Jeremiah 29:12–13).

Through Worship Music

Singing or listening to worship music is a powerful way to connect with God. The lyrics can remind you of His promises and fill you with peace (Colossians 3:16). Sometimes, a song might speak directly to your heart, showing you that God's love is right there with you. These moments bring you closer to God and help you feel His presence.

Through Loving Thoughts

God can place loving thoughts in your mind, like little whispers of encouragement that make you feel loved and valued. These thoughts might bring comfort, courage, or peace right when you need it. When that happens, it can be God helping you remember His love and how much He cares for you (Psalm 94:19).

Through Nature

God's creation is filled with signs of His love. A rainbow after a storm, sunlight shining through the trees, or a butterfly fluttering past you can all be gentle reminders that He's near (Romans 1:20; Psalm 19:1–2). Sometimes, God might use moments like these to comfort your heart and remind you that you're not alone (Matthew 6:26).

Through a Feeling of Peace

When you make a good choice or trust God during a tough time, you might feel a deep sense of peace inside. It's like a calm feeling that settles over you, letting you know you've done the right thing or that you're going to be okay (Philippians 4:7). This peace is God's way of showing you that He's with you and will take care of you.

Through Life Lessons

When hard things happen, God can use them to help you grow. You might learn patience, forgiveness, or how to trust Him more (James 1:2–3). It might not feel like love at the time, but later you may see that God was showing you love through His guidance. These life lessons help shape you into the person He made you to be, helping you become stronger, wiser, and closer to Him.

What to Remember

God's love isn't based on how you feel. It's based on who He is, and He is love (1 John 4:8). Even if your feelings change, His love for you stays the same.

When you feel unsure about God's love, remind yourself of the promises He's made in His Word. God loves you more than you could ever imagine, and nothing in all of creation can take His love away.

TALK ABOUT IT

1. Which of the ways God shows His love do you notice most in your life right now?

2. How can remembering God's promises in the Bible help you trust His love even when you don't feel it?

3. What's one thing in your life that helps you remember how much God cares about you?

Chapter 19

Will God Ever Stop Loving Me?

Have you ever wondered if God might stop loving you? Maybe you made a huge mistake, or you're feeling far from Him and start to worry that His love isn't there anymore. That's a scary thought, but it's something God has already given us the answer to.

God's Love Never Ends

The Bible tells us over and over that God's love will never end. It's not like a battery that runs out of power. It's the biggest, strongest, most powerful force in the universe. Nothing you do can ever make God stop loving you (Lamentations 3:22–23).

God proved His love by sending Jesus to die for us. He didn't wait for us to be perfect. He loved us even when we were at our worst.

The apostle Paul wrote:

> "For I am convinced that neither death nor life,
> neither angels nor demons,
> neither the present nor the future,
> nor any powers, neither height nor depth,
> nor anything else in all creation,
> will be able to separate us from the love of God
> that is in Christ Jesus our Lord."
> — Romans 8:38–39

That means nothing, absolutely nothing, can take God's love away from you.

Imagine a hug that never ends, a flame that never burns out, or a mountain that never moves. That's how strong and steady God's love is.

God Loves You Even When You Mess Up

We all make mistakes. Sometimes we even choose to do things we know are wrong. Thankfully, God's love isn't based on how good we are. He doesn't love us less when we mess up, and He doesn't love us more when we do everything right (Titus 3:4–5).

God doesn't ignore our sins, but He always offers forgiveness. He wants us to come to Him, say we're sorry, and let Him help us grow.

Think about a loving parent. If a child spills something or makes a bad choice, that parent still loves them. They help clean up the mess and teach the child how to do better.

That's what God does for us. The Bible teaches that He can use our mistakes to make us stronger and help shape us into who He created us to be.

God Is Always Near

Sometimes you may feel distant from God. Maybe you've been too busy to pray, or life has been really hard and you don't feel Him near. But the truth is, God never leaves you. He's always close, waiting for you with open arms (James 4:8).

It's kind of like playing a game of hide-and-seek you can't win. Even if you feel lost or hidden, God always knows exactly where you are. It's not because He's playing a game, but because His love never stops seeking you.

Even when you don't feel close to Him, He is close to you. Talking to God, reading the Bible, and remembering His promises help you see that He's always by your side. His love doesn't depend on your feelings. It stays the same no matter what.

What to Remember

If you ever wonder whether God will stop loving you, the answer is simple. No. Never. Not even for a moment.

God loves you on your best days, and He loves you on your worst days. His love doesn't depend on how you feel or what you've done. No mistake, no sin, no emotion, and no failure can ever take it away.

God's love is like the sun. Even when clouds cover it, it keeps shining. His love is constant, strong, and always there for you.

TALK ABOUT IT

1. How does it make you feel to know that nothing can separate you from God's love?

2. Can you think of a time when you sinned but were reminded that God still loves you?

3. What's one way you can remember God's never-ending love when you start to doubt it?

Chapter 20

Can God Forgive Me for Anything?

Have you ever done something that made you feel really bad inside? Maybe you told a lie to stay out of trouble or took something that didn't belong to you. All of us have sinned by disobeying God's rules, and that can leave us feeling ashamed or guilty. But the good news is that God's forgiveness is even greater than our worst choices.

What Is Forgiveness?

Forgiveness means choosing not to stay angry or hold a grudge when someone does something wrong. It's like wiping a messy chalkboard completely clean, with no trace of what was there before.

We can forgive others, and we can ask for forgiveness too. But only God can completely erase our sins and make our hearts clean again. That's why we need Jesus.

Why We Need Jesus to Be Forgiven

To be forgiven by God, we need a Savior. Because God is holy, sin separates us from Him. The Bible says the punishment for sin is death (Romans 6:23), separation from God forever. That's how serious sin is to Him.

But God didn't leave us stuck in our sin. He loves us so much that He sent His Son Jesus to rescue us. Jesus lived a perfect, sinless life, then chose to take the punishment for our sins by dying in our place. Three days later, He rose from the dead, proving His power over sin and death.

To help you picture what Jesus did, think of it like this. Imagine you broke your friend's really expensive toy. You feel awful and you know you'll have to pay for it. But then, someone else steps in and says, "I'll pay for the toy." That's what Jesus did for us. He paid the price for our sins, so we wouldn't have to.

Because of what Jesus did, we don't have to be separated from God anymore (Ephesians 1:7). When we ask Him to forgive us, He doesn't just erase our sin. He gives us a fresh start, as if it never happened (Isaiah 1:18). Through Jesus, we can be completely forgiven and live forever with Him.

No Sin Too Big

The Bible also tells us that no sin is too big for God to forgive.

The apostle John wrote:

> "If we confess our sins,
> he is faithful and just and will forgive us our sins
> and purify us from all unrighteousness."
> — 1 John 1:9

That means even if you've done something that feels really bad, God will still forgive you when you come to Him, confess your sin, and turn away from it.

People in the Bible made bad choices too, and God still forgave them. King David lied, stole, and hurt others. But when he truly repented, God forgave him (2 Samuel 12:13; Psalm 51). The apostle Paul used to persecute Christians, which means he treated them badly and tried to stop them from following Jesus. After meeting Jesus, he was forgiven and became one of the greatest messengers of the Gospel (Acts 7:58; 9:1–22; 1 Timothy 1:13–16).

How Do We Receive Forgiveness?

God forgives us because of Jesus' sacrifice on the cross. To receive that forgiveness, there are three things you need to do:

1. **Confess Your Sins:** Tell God what you've done wrong. He already knows everything, but He wants you to be honest about it and come to Him with a sincere heart (1 John 1:9).

2. **Repent:** This means turning away from your sin and turning to Jesus for help and forgiveness (Acts 3:19). It's more than just saying "I'm sorry." Repentance means that you don't want to keep sinning. You want Jesus to change your heart and help you live God's way.

3. **Follow Jesus:** True faith isn't just believing that Jesus exists. It means trusting Him as your Lord and Savior.

Even demons believe that God exists, but they don't follow Him (James 2:19). Real faith means loving Jesus with your whole heart and choosing to obey His commands (John 14:15).

Forgiveness and Healing

When God forgives you, it brings peace to your heart. His grace lifts the weight of your guilt and replaces it with love.

Imagine carrying a backpack full of heavy rocks. Each rock represents a bad choice you've made. When God forgives you, He takes that heavy weight off your shoulders, making you feel lighter. Psalm 103:12 says that God takes our sins away and separates them from us as far as the east is from the west.

But forgiveness doesn't just free you from guilt. It also helps you grow. When you receive God's mercy, it changes your heart and leads you to make better choices.

Forgiving Others

Jesus told us to forgive others just as God forgives us.

He said:

> "For if you forgive other people when they sin against you, your heavenly Father will also forgive you."
> — Matthew 6:14

Forgiving someone doesn't mean pretending nothing happened. It means choosing to let go of anger and show kindness, just like God does for us. Holding onto anger hurts your heart. Forgiveness helps heal the hurt inside of you and it shows God's love to others.

God's Love Never Ends

God's love and forgiveness never run out. He's always ready to forgive anyone who comes to Him with a sincere heart. His grace flows like a river that never runs dry, and no sin is too big for His love.

Even when you feel far from Him, God welcomes you back with open arms (Luke 15:20). He will never stop loving you or calling you back to His heart.

What to Remember

God's forgiveness is a gift. You don't have to earn it. You just need to come to Him with a heart that wants to change.

When you confess your sins, turn away from them, and trust in Jesus, God forgives you completely. He removes your guilt, fills you with peace, and gives you a brand-new start.

When you mess up, God will never turn away from you. No matter what you've done, you will always be loved.

TALK ABOUT IT

1. How does it make you feel to know that no sin is too big for God to forgive?

2. Can you think of a time when you asked God for forgiveness and felt peace afterward?

3. What's one way you can practice forgiveness toward others, even if it feels hard?

Chapter 21

Why Does God Give Us Rules?

Imagine playing a game without any rules. It would be confusing, wouldn't it? Everyone would be doing different things, and the game wouldn't work very well. In the same way, God gives us rules to help us live happy, safe, and meaningful lives. These rules aren't meant to be harsh or take away our fun. They're like helpful instructions that show us the best way to live.

What Are God's Rules?

A long time ago, after God rescued the Israelites from slavery in Egypt, He brought them to a mountain called Mount Sinai. There, God gave Moses a special set of rules called the Ten Commandments (Exodus 20). Moses was the man God chose to guide the people of Israel and help them follow His ways.

These commandments were written on stone tablets by God Himself and given to His people to help them live the right way. And they're still important today because they teach us right from wrong and how to treat God and others.

Here's what the Ten Commandments teach:

1. Put God first by loving and trusting Him more than anything else.

2. Don't make or worship idols or put anything above God.

3. Respect God's name and speak of Him with honor.

4. Take one day of the week to rest and spend time with God. This is called the Sabbath.

5. Honor your father and mother by respecting them.

6. Do not murder, which means taking someone's life on purpose.

7. Keep yourself pure and be faithful in marriage.

8. Don't steal by taking something that doesn't belong to you.

9. Always tell the truth instead of lying.

10. Be thankful for what you have instead of being jealous of others.

These rules are all about love, and they give us a strong foundation for how to live a good life.

But God didn't stop there. The Ten Commandments aren't the only rules He's given us. Throughout the Bible, He gives more instructions that help us live in ways that honor Him and bless others. Many of those instructions come through the life and teachings of Jesus.

The Bible says:

"For the LORD gives wisdom;
from His mouth come knowledge and understanding."
— Proverbs 2:6

God's Rules Help Us Love Well

When someone asked Jesus what the most important commandment was, He didn't choose one from the list of Ten Commandments. Instead, He gave an answer that sums up the heart behind all of God's laws.

Jesus said the greatest commandment is to love the Lord your God with all your heart, with all your soul, and with all your mind. The second is to love your neighbor as yourself (Matthew 22:36–40).

Every one of God's commandments helps us grow in love. Rules like being kind, honest, and forgiving help us show love to other people. Rules about prayer and worship help us show love to God. When we follow God's rules, we're showing that we care about Him and the people around us.

Rules Keep Us Safe and Lead to Good Things

God's rules are like guardrails on the road. They protect us and others from getting hurt. For example, rules against lying, stealing, or being unkind help make our world safer and more peaceful.

Just like a parent sets rules to protect their children, God gives us rules to guard us and lead us in the right direction (Deuteronomy 6:24). Even when we don't fully understand why, we can trust that His rules come from love.

Think about wearing a seatbelt. When you're little, it might seem uncomfortable or unnecessary. But parents insist on it because they know it keeps you safe. It's the same with God's rules. They aren't meant to get in your way. They're designed to keep you safe and lead you into a life that's truly good.

God's Rules Make Us Strong

God's rules also help us grow in character. Following His ways builds strength on the inside.

When you practice patience, you learn how to stay calm under pressure. When you choose to share, you grow a generous heart. And when you tell the truth, even when it's hard, you learn to be trustworthy.

These habits help shape you into the person God made you to be (Hebrews 12:11). He wants you to grow into the best version of yourself.

Rules and Forgiveness

No one follows God's rules perfectly. And even when we mess up, God's love and grace are always there.

When we break His rules and truly feel sorry for what we've done, we can ask Him to forgive us, and He will (1 John 1:9). He doesn't hold our sins against us. Instead, He helps us learn from them and grow stronger.

God's rules aren't meant to punish us. They're meant to guide us. And when we fall short, His love gives us a fresh start every time.

What to Remember

God gives us rules because He loves us. His rules show us how to love Him and others, keep us safe, and help us grow. Even if we don't understand all of them, we can trust that His wisdom is greater than ours.

And when we do mess up, God is always ready to forgive us and help us begin again. Following His rules shows that we trust His heart and want to walk in His ways. That's when life becomes full of purpose, direction, and lasting peace.

TALK ABOUT IT

1. Which of God's rules feels most meaningful to you right now, and why?

2. Can you think of a rule that helps keep people safe or shows love to others?

3. How does it make you feel to know that even when you break God's rules, He offers you forgiveness and a fresh start?

Part 4

Dealing with Doubts and Sharing Faith

Chapter 22

How Do I Tell My Friends About Jesus?

It's natural to want to share good things with your friends, like your favorite games, a funny movie, or a delicious snack. When you discover how amazing Jesus is, it makes sense to want to share Him too. But sometimes, talking about Jesus can feel scary or awkward. You might wonder, *What if it sounds weird? What if they don't understand?* Don't worry. There are plenty of gentle ways to talk about Jesus without pressure or fear.

Pray First

Before you tell your friends about Jesus, talk to God and ask for His help. He will prepare your heart and remind you that you're never sharing your faith alone.

Prayer might feel tricky at times, but these ideas can help you get started:

- **Pray for Their Hearts:** Ask God to help your friends feel His love and discover the truth about Him. Pray that they would come to know Him personally and want to follow Him.

- **Pray for Opportunities:** Ask God to arrange moments for you to talk about Him. These could come through simple conversations, kind actions, or inviting a friend to church. God wants to give you plenty of chances to share His love with others.

- **Pray for Yourself:** It's normal to feel nervous about sharing your faith, but God will help you when you ask. Pray for courage, wisdom, and for the right words to say (Colossians 4:6). He promises to be with you and help you share from your heart.

Live Out Your Faith

You don't always need words to share your faith. Sometimes, your actions speak the loudest. When the way you live matches what you believe, people will notice.

Here are a few ways to live out your faith:

- **Be a Good Friend:** One of the easiest ways to share your faith is by being a friend others can count on. Be kind, encouraging, and willing to help when someone's in need. If you're known for being thoughtful and caring, your friends may wonder what makes you different. That's a great time to talk about Jesus.

- **Show Respect:** Not everyone will believe the same things you do, and that can feel hard sometimes. But when you treat others with kindness, even when you disagree, you show them that Christianity is about grace, not judgment.

- **Be Honest:** Telling the truth and doing what's right helps people trust you. When your actions match your words, your faith becomes something others can see. This kind of honesty shows others that following Jesus makes a real difference in your life (Philippians 2:15).

- **Be Forgiving:** Everyone makes mistakes. When your friends hurt your feelings, choose to forgive them. This shows God's love in action (Ephesians 4:32), and it may lead your friends to ask why you're so patient and kind. That gives you a meaningful chance to explain your faith.

Be Ready to Talk

You don't need to be an expert to talk about Jesus. Just be real and willing to share what He means to you.

Here's how:

- **Listen First:** If a friend is struggling, be a good listener. Sometimes, showing that you care is the best way to prepare someone's heart to hear about God.

- **Keep It Simple:** You don't need big words or fancy answers. You could say something like, "Jesus is God's Son. He died for my sins and rose again so I can be close to God."

- **Share Your Story:** Talk about how Jesus has helped you. Maybe He gave you peace when you were afraid, carried you through something hard, or helped you become a kinder person. Whatever your story is, it's powerful, and it can encourage others.

- **Answer Questions Honestly:** If someone asks you a question you don't know how to answer, it's okay to say, "I'm not sure, but I can find out." Then look for the answer and share it with them later. That shows honesty and can keep the conversation going.

Invite, Don't Pressure

Sharing your beliefs should feel like you're offering a gift, not forcing someone to take it. People respond better to love than to pressure.

Here are a few simple ways to invite your friends to learn more about Jesus:

- **Invite Them to Church:** If your church has a fun event or special service, invite your friends to come. They might enjoy it even if they don't believe in God yet.

- **Share What You Love:** If you enjoy a worship song, Christian book, or faith-filled movie, share it! Sometimes, music or stories speak to people's hearts in a way that regular words can't.

- **Be Patient:** Faith takes time. Some friends may be interested in learning about God right away, while others might not be ready yet. That's when patience and prayer matter most. Keep being a good friend and trust that God is working in their hearts (1 Corinthians 3:6).

Remember Who Does the Changing

At the end of the day, it's not your job to change someone's heart. That part belongs to God. Your job is to be faithful by loving others, living like Jesus, and sharing the truth.

And if your friends don't believe right away, don't lose hope. God is always working, even when you can't see it. Every kind word, every small act of love, and every prayer matters. Keep being a light in their lives, and trust God to do the rest.

What to Remember

Talking to your friends about Jesus doesn't have to feel scary. When you pray with a caring heart, live out your faith, and look for chances to talk about Him, God can use you in big ways.

You don't need to be perfect. You just need to be faithful. Keep showing God's love and trust Him with what happens next. Remember, when you share the good news about Jesus, you're helping someone find the way to God.

TALK ABOUT IT

1. What's one way you could show Jesus' love to a friend without using words?

2. How would you explain Jesus to a friend who asked about Him?

3. What's one simple way you could start a conversation about Jesus without it feeling scary?

Chapter 23

Is It Okay to Have Doubts About God?

Have you ever looked up at the night sky and felt tiny compared to the stars? Maybe you've wondered, *Is God really out there?* Or maybe someone told you there's no proof of God, and it made you start to question things. If you've ever had thoughts like that, you're not alone. Many people have doubts sometimes, even strong Christians.

Doubts Are Just Questions That Need Answers

It's normal to have doubts, and it doesn't mean you're doing anything wrong. In fact, doubt can be a sign that you're thinking carefully about your faith. It's like learning something new in school. You ask questions so you can understand better, right?

Your questions matter, and they deserve honest, thoughtful answers (Jude 1:22).

Why Do People Doubt?

Doubts don't just show up for no reason. They usually grow from something we see, hear, or experience.

Here are a few reasons people start to question their faith:

Hard Things Happen

Life doesn't always make sense, and it's okay to wonder about it. *Why do bad things happen to good people? Why does God let people suffer?* When someone we love gets sick or something unfair happens, it's natural to ask, "Where is God?"

They Hear Confusing Things

Maybe someone told you that science proves God isn't real or that the Bible is just a made-up story. That can feel confusing, especially if they sound sure about it. But just because someone says something doesn't mean it's true.

They Think Deep Thoughts

Sometimes our minds wander into big ideas. *Where did everything come from? What happens after we die?* These are honest, important questions, and wondering about them shows you're thinking with care.

How Do We Find Answers?

Doubt isn't the opposite of faith. It's part of how your faith grows. The key is not to ignore your questions, but to look for the truth.

Here are some ways to do that:

Pray

Tell God what you're feeling. Ask Him to help you believe, especially if your faith feels shaky. You don't need to hide your doubts from Him. He already knows them. In the Bible, a man once asked Jesus to help him believe because he was struggling with unbelief (Mark 9:24). You can pray like that too. When you bring your questions to God and keep seeking Him, He will guide you to the truth (Matthew 7:7).

Talk to Grownups You Trust

Ask your parents, your pastor, or a trusted Christian adult for help. Chances are, they've had doubts too. They can share what helped them, offer encouragement, and help you understand things better.

Read the Bible

The Bible is full of stories about people who had doubts. Some of them even questioned God directly (Habakkuk 1:2). But as they got to know Him, their faith became stronger. The more you read the Bible, the more you'll understand who God is, and the more confident you'll feel in your faith.

Be Part of a Church

Church is a place where you can grow, learn, and ask questions without feeling alone. Being around other believers can help you stay strong when you're unsure about things. Churches can differ in how they teach and understand the Bible, so it's important to find one that follows it faithfully. Look for a Christian church that believes Jesus is the Son of God who died and rose again. A good church helps you grow through prayer, worship, and learning God's Word together.

Look for Proof

God doesn't expect you to believe without any reason. There's real, powerful evidence that points to His existence. From science to history, there are tons of clues that support Christianity. The Bible itself is backed by archaeology, eyewitness accounts, and historical documents (2 Peter 1:16). You don't need to have blind faith. God gives us good reasons to trust Him.

Books That Help You Believe

Looking for evidence is like solving a big mystery. There are so many clues that point to God. If you love asking questions and want to explore more, these books are great for kids like you:

- **Case for Christ for Kids**
  by Lee Strobel
  Discover the evidence for Jesus' life, death, and resurrection in a way that's easy to understand.

- **Case for a Creator for Kids**
  by Lee Strobel
  Learn how science points to a Creator through DNA, the universe, and other clues in nature.

- **Cold-Case Christianity for Kids**
  by J. Warner Wallace
  Use real detective skills to explore the truth about Christianity by looking at evidence for Jesus and the Bible.

- **God's Crime Scene for Kids**
  by J. Warner Wallace
  Search for clues in the world around you. From the stars to your body, everything points to a Creator.

What to Remember

Doubts don't mean your faith is broken. They're a chance for your faith to grow.

Asking questions can help you find the answers you're looking for. God isn't afraid of your doubts. He welcomes your questions and invites you to keep seeking Him.

The more you explore, the more you'll discover that Christianity is true. God is real, loving, and always ready to meet you right where you are.

TALK ABOUT IT

1. What's one big question about God or faith that you've had before?

2. When you feel doubts about God, who is one trusted person you could talk to about them?

3. How does it help to know that God welcomes your questions and isn't afraid of your doubts?

Chapter 24

Why Doesn't God Allow Us to Understand Everything?

Have you ever asked a question, only to hear, "I don't know" or "It's complicated"? Maybe it was something really important, and you wished someone had the answer. Unfortunately, even the smartest people in the world don't know everything. Sometimes we wish God would just explain it all to us. Wouldn't life be easier if we had all the answers?

But God, in His perfect wisdom, reveals things at just the right time and in just the right way. We won't always understand why, but we can trust that He has a reason for everything He chooses to show us, and everything He doesn't.

God Sees the Whole Picture

Imagine listening to an orchestra as the musicians tune their instruments before a concert. The sounds clash and feel messy, like a bunch of random notes. But the conductor isn't worried. He knows that soon, it will become a beautiful symphony.

That's how it is with God. He sees the whole story of the world, from beginning to end, and how it all fits together. We only see a tiny part, so things might feel confusing or out of place.

Learning to Trust God's Timing

Sometimes, God doesn't tell us everything because it's not the right time, or we're not ready to understand yet. He helps us grow little by little, giving us only what we're ready for instead of too much at once (John 16:12).

The Bible also tells us that some things are mysteries, parts of God's plan He keeps hidden for a reason (Deuteronomy 29:29). But mysteries don't have to be bad or scary. Think about a wrapped present. You don't know what's inside yet, but when the time is right, you get to open it. In the same way, some things stay hidden until God chooses to show them. And His timing is always perfect.

Growing in Faith

When things don't make sense, it gives us a chance to grow in our faith. Faith means trusting God even when we don't see the whole picture. It's like using a flashlight in the dark. You can only see a few steps ahead, but that's enough to keep moving forward.

The Bible says to trust God with all your heart (Proverbs 3:5–6). That means trusting Him even when you have questions, even when life feels hard, and even when you don't understand what He's doing. It's okay to ask questions. But it's important to remember that God is in control, and His way is always best.

Asking for Wisdom

Wisdom means knowing how to make good choices and understanding right from wrong.

The Bible says:

> "If any of you lacks wisdom, you should ask God,
> who gives generously to all without finding fault,
> and it will be given to you."
> — James 1:5

God doesn't expect us to figure everything out on our own. When we ask Him for help, He teaches us how to think, how to respond, and how to trust Him.

What to Remember

We're never going to have all the answers, but we can choose to trust God.

When life feels confusing, we can remember that God sees more than we do, knows more than we know, and gives us exactly what we need to take each step in our journey.

He's already revealed His heart through Jesus. And even though we still have questions, we're never alone in them. God walks with us, teaches us, and leads us one step at a time.

Our job isn't to figure everything out. It's to follow the One who already has.

TALK ABOUT IT

1. How does it feel to know that God sees the whole picture of your life even when you can only see a small part?

2. What's one question you have for God that you don't fully understand right now?

3. How can trusting God's wisdom help you when things in life feel confusing?

Part 5

Facing Life's Hard Moments

.

Chapter 25

Why Does God Allow Suffering?

Life can be really hard sometimes. People get sick, loved ones pass away, and some kids don't have enough food to eat. When you see things like that, you might wonder, *If God is so good and powerful, why does He let these things happen?* There isn't one simple answer, but the Bible shows us what to remember when life hurts.

God Gave Us the Freedom to Choose

God created people with free will, which means we get to make our own choices (Deuteronomy 30:19). This is a good thing because it lets us experience real love, including love for God, love for others, and love for ourselves. We can choose to love our families, be kind to strangers, and live in a way that honors the Lord.

Imagine a world where everyone was programmed like robots to always do what's right. There might be no suffering, but there wouldn't be real love either, because love must be chosen freely. God didn't make us like robots. He made us His children, with the ability to choose love (Joshua 24:15).

That kind of freedom makes real love possible, but it also opens the door to real pain.

When people misuse their free will, it creates a ripple effect of consequences. It's like dropping a rock into a pond and watching the waves spread out in every direction. One person's bad choice can affect many others, leading to pain that feels unfair. And when you're the one getting hurt, it can feel even worse. But only through true freedom can we experience the depth of love.

When the Whole World Hurts

You might hear about big and painful things happening around the world, like homelessness, earthquakes, or starvation, and wonder where God is in all of it. These things can be hard to understand, even for adults.

The Bible tells us that sin has broken the world, and that's a big reason why so many things feel wrong or unfair (Genesis 3). When Adam and Eve disobeyed God in the Garden of Eden, sin entered the world like a sickness. It spread into everything, even nature. That's why we have things like disease, disasters, and even war.

You might wonder, *Why do we have to suffer because of something Adam and Eve did?*

Here's one way to think about it. Imagine building a tall tower on a cracked foundation. If the base is broken, the whole structure eventually falls apart. That one moment in the garden caused things to break across the entire Earth, and we still see the results today.

But thankfully, God hasn't left us alone. He sees every person, every struggle, and every tear. And He promises that one day, Jesus will return to make everything new again (Revelation 21:4). Until that day comes, God calls us to care for those who are hurting and to shine His light in the darkness (Matthew 5:16).

God's Purpose and Presence in Suffering

Hard times never feel good. When you're hurting, you just want the pain to stop. You might ask God to fix everything and wonder why He hasn't. But God sees more than we do. Even when life feels unfair, He still has a plan. His ways are higher than ours (Isaiah 55:9). That means even when we don't understand what's happening, we can trust that He's working behind the scenes.

Jesus said:

> "I have told you these things,
> so that in me you may have peace.
> In this world you will have trouble.
> But take heart! I have overcome the world."
> — John 16:33

God can use even the hardest moments to help us grow. Just like a seed has to die before it can grow into something new, He can bring life out of the times that hurt us the most (John 12:24). Suffering can make us stronger, more caring, and more dependent on Him.

And we're never alone in our pain. Jesus understands suffering because He went through it too. Jesus was betrayed, beaten, nailed to a cross, and died because of it. But He didn't stay dead. He rose again, and that gives us hope that pain and sadness won't last forever. When we're hurting or scared, we can always talk to God in prayer, knowing that He listens and cares.

Remember, this world is not our forever home. One day, in Heaven, there will be no more pain, no more tears, and no more suffering. God doesn't enjoy our pain, but He promises that something better is coming.

How to Cope with Suffering

When something really bad happens, it can feel like your whole world is upside down. You might feel sad, scared, or even confused. But you don't have to face it alone.

Here are some simple ways to help your heart feel stronger when life gets tough:

- **Talk to a Trusted Adult:** Share your feelings with a parent, teacher, or pastor. Talking things out with someone who cares can be a big relief.

- **Pray:** Talk to God about your pain and ask for His comfort. Even if you don't know what to say, He understands how you feel.

- **Read the Bible:** Look for stories of hope and encouragement. They can bring you comfort and remind you that you're never alone.

- **Help Others:** Doing something kind for someone else

can help you feel better too. It shows you that you can still make a difference, even in hard times.

- **Remember God's Love:** Even in the toughest moments, God's love for you never changes. His love is steady, strong, and always with you.

What to Remember

It's okay to ask questions when life feels hard. Even Jesus cried out to God and asked "why" when He was suffering (Matthew 27:46).

We won't always understand why bad things happen, but that doesn't mean God isn't good. He still loves us, He's still in control, and He promises to be with us no matter what.

So when life is confusing, talk to God about it. He cares about your pain, and He can use even the hardest moments for something good.

TALK ABOUT IT

1. How does it help you to know that Jesus understands suffering because He went through it too?

2. When you see pain in the world, what's one way you can show God's love to someone who's hurting?

3. What gives you hope when life feels unfair or confusing?

Chapter 26

Why Do Bad Things Happen to Good People?

When life feels unfair, it can stir up some really big thoughts. Maybe someone you love got really sick, or a storm damaged your home or school. In moments like this, life doesn't just feel unfair, it feels wrong.

You might wonder, *Why would God allow things like this to happen to people who don't deserve it?* This is a big thing to think about, and even adults struggle with it.

It's important to know that God welcomes our questions. He doesn't get upset when we feel confused or ask about these things. He listens with love and truly cares how our hearts are feeling.

The World Is Broken, and It Hurts

When God first created the world, it was perfect. There was no suffering, no death, and nothing went wrong (Genesis 1:31). But the Bible tells us that Adam and Eve made a choice to disobey God. And when they did, sin entered the world (Genesis 3).

Sin didn't just mean people started doing bad things, it broke everything. The world itself became a place where pain, sadness, and tragedy exist.

That's why terrible things happen. Not because God wants them to, but because the world isn't how it was meant to be. Bad things can happen to people, and we can't always find a reason why. It's not because someone deserved it, or because God was punishing them, or that He didn't care.

Sometimes awful things happen simply because the world is broken.

Did God Let This Happen?

It's okay to wonder, *Couldn't God have stopped it?* The truth is, yes, He could have. God is all-powerful. He could stop every accident, every sickness, and every tragedy. So why doesn't He?

This is one of the hardest questions ever asked, and we may not fully understand the answer until we get to Heaven. But the Bible tells us that God is love (1 John 4:8). That means He's never careless or cruel. Even though He allows pain, it's not because He wants to hurt us.

God gave us something called free will. That means we have the ability to make our own choices. And for love to be real, it has to be freely chosen. But if we're free to choose love, we're also free to choose sin. That's part of why the world is so broken. This kind of freedom can be hard to understand, especially when it leads to pain.

Imagine a loving parent teaching their child to ride a bike. The parent could hold on forever to make sure the child never falls. But then the child would never learn or grow. Letting go is scary, but it's part of the process.

It's the same with God. He gives us the freedom to ride, but He's always close by, ready to help us get back up.

When God Feels Silent

One of God's prophets, named Habakkuk, once cried out to God because he saw righteous people suffering in a world that felt cruel and broken. He asked how long things would stay this way and why God seemed silent through it all (Habakkuk 1:2–4).

God answered Habakkuk and said:

> "For I am going to do something in your days
> that you would not believe,
> even if you were told."
> — Habakkuk 1:5

God didn't explain everything right away. But He reminded Habakkuk that He was still working, even when it didn't look like it. This helps us know that when God feels silent, He is not absent.

Even Jesus Suffered

When we're hurting, it can be easy to wonder if God really understands. But He does. Jesus suffered too.

Jesus is God in human form. He knew what it felt like to be tired, rejected, mocked, and even betrayed by people He loved. And when He was dying on the cross, He cried out:

"My God, my God,
why have you forsaken me?"
— Matthew 27:46

Jesus didn't deserve any of the pain He experienced. It didn't seem fair, and it didn't seem right. God didn't desire that suffering, but He allowed it. Then God used that terrible moment to bring about something good, the greatest good the world has ever seen. Jesus' suffering led to our salvation.

That doesn't mean every bad thing will turn into something good. Some things are just tragic. But it does mean that God is never absent in our pain. He understands it, and He can bring healing even when life feels impossible.

The Bible says:

> "The LORD is close to the brokenhearted
> and saves those who are crushed in spirit."
> — Psalm 34:18

That means He's close to us in our sadness, in our pain, and in our questions. God can even use the hardest moments in our lives to help us grow. He shapes us, strengthens us, and teaches us to hold on when life gets tough.

Hope for the Future

God has promised that one day, all pain and sadness will end. There will be no more sickness, no more suffering, and no more death. The Bible says that God Himself will comfort His people and wipe away every tear. Everything that's broken will be made new (Revelation 21:4).

That means all the hurt we've felt, whether from sickness, loss, fear, or confusion, won't last forever. God cares every time you cry and knows your every sorrow. One day, He will make everything right.

Until then, we hold on to hope. We may not understand everything, but we can trust that God is always good, and He's always with us.

What to Remember

Bad things happen to good people, not because God wants them to, but because the world is broken. This isn't how God meant it to be. When sin entered the world, pain and suffering came with it. We don't always understand why something happens, but it's not because someone deserved it or because God didn't care.

Even in our hardest moments, God is still here, and He is still good. He shows us His love, helps us grow, and gives us strength. And one day, all the pain will be gone, and we'll understand how He was with us through it all.

TALK ABOUT IT

1. How does it make you feel to know that bad things happen because the world is broken, not because God doesn't care?

2. How can God help you grow during hard times?

3. When life feels painful, what's something you can do to remember that God is still with you?

Chapter 27

Why Are Some Babies Born Sick or with a Disability?

It can be heartbreaking to see a baby born with serious health problems or special needs. You might wonder, *If God is so loving, how could He let an innocent baby suffer?* That question is painful, and there isn't always a clear answer.

But even in the middle of these challenges, we can remember that every child is created by God, deeply loved, and never forgotten. God stays close to us when we're hurting, and He gives meaning to every life.

What the Bible Says

The Bible doesn't explain everything, but it does help guide us through the pain.

Here are some important things to remember when a baby is born with health challenges:

The World Is Broken

The Bible tells us that the world is no longer perfect. When sin entered the world through Adam and Eve, brokenness followed, including sickness, disease, and disabilities (Romans 5:12). These things don't happen because God wants them to, but because we live in a world that's been broken by sin.

God's Ways Are Higher

The Bible also tells us that God's ways are much greater than ours (Isaiah 55:9). Just like a child doesn't always understand a parent's decision, we don't always understand what God allows. This doesn't mean God causes sickness or disabilities, but He may allow them for reasons we can't see yet.

God Can Bring Good from Challenges

Even in difficult situations, God can bring beauty and meaning (Romans 8:28). A baby's illness or disability can unite people in love and compassion, strengthen family bonds, and even lead others to God.

God's Unique Design

Every person is created with purpose (Psalm 139:13–14). What the world calls a disability, God may see as a special way for His love to shine. Many people with disabilities show great courage and inspire others. God values each person, not for how they look or what they can do, but for who they are on the inside.

Some Things Won't Make Sense Until Heaven

Some questions won't be answered in this life. We don't always understand why God lets certain things happen, but the Bible reminds us to keep trusting Him.

> "Trust in the Lᴏʀᴅ with all your heart
> and lean not on your own understanding."
> — Proverbs 3:5

One day in Heaven, we may finally understand what didn't make sense here on Earth. Until then, we can hold on to our faith and trust that God is always good, even when life is hard.

Finding Comfort and Showing Love

If you know a baby who is sick or has a disability, here are some ways you can show care and find comfort:

- **Pray**: Talk to God about the baby and their family. Ask Him to bring them healing, strength, and peace. Even when we don't understand what's happening, we can trust that God hears us and cares.

- **Be Kind and Supportive**: A kind word or thoughtful action can mean a lot to families going through a hard time. Look for ways to show love and respect to them, because every life is precious to God.

- **Learn and Understand**: The more we learn about disabilities and health challenges, the easier it is to care. When we understand more, we can be even better friends and helpers.

- **Trust God's Plan**: Life won't always make sense, but God's love never changes. He sees every child, knows every story, and has a plan for every life, no matter what it looks like.

What to Remember

It's never easy when a baby is born sick or with a disability. It's okay to feel sad, confused, or full of questions. But we're never alone in those feelings. God sees our pain and stays close when we're hurting. He understands our sadness and offers comfort when we turn to Him.

Even when we don't understand why something happens, we can still trust that God is good. He loves us and has a plan for every person. Life on Earth may be hard, but we can still show love, kindness, and acceptance to those who need support.

God's love is bigger than anything we can imagine. And one day, He will give His children new heavenly bodies that are free from pain, sickness, and every kind of struggle.

TALK ABOUT IT

1. How does it make you feel to know that every child is created by God and deeply loved, no matter what their health or abilities are?

2. What's one way you could show kindness or support to a family who has a baby with special needs?

3. How does knowing that God will one day make all things new give you hope when life feels confusing or sad?

Chapter 28

Why Does Life Seem Unfair?

Has something ever happened that didn't go the way it should, and you found yourself saying, "That's not fair"? Maybe you studied hard for a test but still got a bad grade, while someone else barely tried and got an A. Or maybe someone you love is really sick, and nothing seems to help them feel better.

Some unfair things are small, like a bad grade. But others feel much bigger, like when a kind person has a serious illness, even though they did nothing to deserve it. It's normal to ask why life can be unfair and to wonder where God is in the middle of it. But we need to remember that God's plan is bigger than what we can see. He's always working for our good, even when life doesn't make sense.

God Sees the Bigger Picture

When things don't seem fair, it helps to remember that we don't see the whole story. But God does. Imagine reading a book and stopping in the middle of a sad or scary chapter. If you didn't read to the end, you might think everything turns out badly. But the author knows how the story will end.

Like an author, God is helping to write the story of your life (Psalm 139:16). He sees every moment from start to finish and is working behind the scenes in ways you might not understand yet.

At the same time, God gives people free will, which means they can choose to do what's right or wrong. Sadly, some of those choices bring pain and unfairness into the world. But even then, God is still at work, turning brokenness into something beautiful.

The Bible tells us that what we suffer now isn't the end. The apostle Paul once wrote:

> "I consider that our present sufferings
> are not worth comparing with
> the glory that will be revealed in us."
> — Romans 8:18

God knows life isn't always fair, but He promises that one day, He will set everything right.

God Is Good Even When Life Isn't

It's easy to trust God when life is going well. But what about when it's not?

That's when we need to remember that God is always good, even when life doesn't feel that way.

> "The LORD is good,
> a refuge [a safe place] in times of trouble.
> He cares for those who trust in Him."
> — Nahum 1:7

When unfair things happen, we can run to God for comfort. He never ignores our pain. He walks with us through every hard moment, gives us strength when we feel weak, and reminds us that we're never alone. God's love never changes, and He will never leave us to face struggles on our own.

Unfairness in Money and Belongings

Sometimes unfairness shows up in the things people have. Maybe someone who's mean gets everything they want, while a really nice person struggles just to have enough food. It's easy to wonder why God allows that.

But Jesus told us that what we own on Earth isn't what matters the most. He said not to store up treasures that can be stolen or ruined, but to live for what lasts forever by focusing our hearts on heaven (Matthew 6:19–20).

God also tells us not to let jealousy take over our thoughts. One of the Ten Commandments says not to be jealous of what others have (Exodus 20:17). Instead of wishing for what someone else has, we can trust that God gives us exactly what we need (Philippians 4:19). Real joy doesn't come from toys, clothes, or money. It comes from knowing God and trusting His love.

God's Rewards Are Better Than Fairness

Sometimes, life feels unfair because the world is broken by sin. But this world isn't our forever home.

God sees every kind thing you do. He sees every time you choose to be honest, every moment you keep trusting Him, and every time you do what's right, even when it's hard. God promises that one day, there will be no more pain or sadness (Revelation 21:4). And when that day comes, all the unfairness in this world won't matter anymore.

What to Remember

Life won't always feel fair, but that doesn't mean God isn't in control. He sees the whole story, walks with you through every hard time, and promises that one day everything will be made right.

So when things don't feel fair, remember that God's rewards are greater than anything we might miss out on while we're here on Earth. God is good, His plan is big, and His love for you will never fail.

TALK ABOUT IT

1. How do you usually feel when something unfair happens to you?

2. How does it help to remember that God sees the bigger picture, even when you don't?

3. What's one way you can focus on God's goodness instead of comparing yourself to others?

Chapter 29

Why Doesn't God Stop Bad Things from Happening?

When something bad happens, it's natural to wonder why God didn't stop it. Many people have wrestled with this question for a long time. Maybe you've seen something sad, like a fire that destroyed someone's home or a student who got bullied even though they were kind to everyone. Maybe someone you loved passed away, and you thought, *God could have stopped this. Why didn't He?*

It's okay to ask questions like this. The Bible shows us that God is patient with our doubts and invites us to seek Him when we don't understand (Proverbs 2:3–5; John 20:27). It also helps us understand why bad things happen and how we can still trust God, especially when life hurts.

Why Doesn't He Step In?

One reason pain and trouble exist is because God gave people free will. He allows us to make our own choices, even when those choices cause harm. If God stopped every bad thing before it happened, we wouldn't truly have freedom. We'd only be able to do what He programmed us to do. But love and kindness are only real when they're chosen, not forced. That's why God gives us the ability to choose to love Him and others.

Sadly, people don't always use their free will for good. Some choose to be selfish, angry, or mean, and others get hurt because of it. God doesn't like when we sin, but He allows those decisions because freedom is part of His design for love.

But not all pain is caused by human choices. Things like storms, floods, and earthquakes happen because the world is broken. Sin didn't just affect people. It affected all of creation. While some struggles come from people's actions, others happen simply because the world is no longer perfect. Yet even in those moments, God is still here, and He can use our struggles to help us grow closer to Him (James 1:2–4).

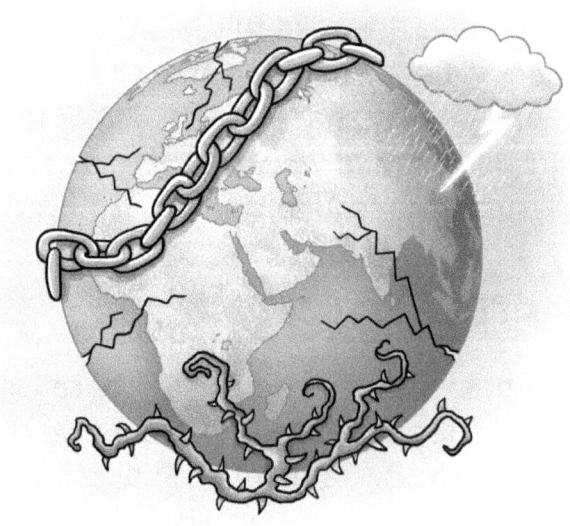

God's Bigger Plan

When bad things happen, it can feel like everything is out of control. We may wonder why God would allow suffering if He has the power to stop it. But the Bible shows that even when things look terrible, God can bring good out of bad situations.

Joseph's life in the Old Testament is a great example. He was hurt by his brothers, sold as a slave into Egypt, and put in prison for something he didn't do. But later, God used Joseph to help save people from starvation during a terrible famine. He was put in charge of all the food in the land and became second in command to Pharaoh, the most powerful leader in Egypt. Joseph said that what others meant for harm, God used for good (Genesis 37–50).

God sees the whole story of life from beginning to end, while we only see one page at a time.

God also promises that He has good plans for His people, even when it feels like life is falling apart.

> "For I know the plans I have for you," declares the LORD,
> "plans to prosper you and not to harm you,
> plans to give you hope and a future."
> — Jeremiah 29:11

This verse was originally a promise to the Israelites when they were forced to leave their homeland, but it shows us God's heart. He is always working for good, whether we can see it or not. Even in hard times, He's preparing something better than we can imagine.

God Cares About Your Pain

When you're hurting, it's important to remember that God isn't far away. He's close, and He understands exactly what you're going through. The Bible calls Him the Father of compassion and the God of all comfort. Like a loving parent who holds their child when they're sad, God comforts us in our troubles so that we can one day help others who are struggling too (2 Corinthians 1:3–4).

Here are some things you can do when you're hurting:

- **Talk to God in Prayer:** Tell Him how you really feel. He hears you, understands your pain, and stays with you through every difficult moment.

- **Read the Bible:** The Bible is full of stories about people who went through hard times and found comfort in God. Reading their stories can help strengthen your faith.

- **Lean on Others:** Reach out to family, friends, or people at church. God often uses those around you to bring support, love, and encouragement. You don't have to face challenges alone.

God's Justice Will Come

Sometimes, life feels unfair. It can be especially hard when people do bad things and seem to get away with it. Maybe someone lied, cheated, or hurt others and never got caught, while someone kind continues to struggle. That doesn't seem right.

But the Bible tells us that God is fair, and nothing gets past Him.

> "Be sure of this: The wicked will not go unpunished,
> but those who are righteous will go free."
> — Proverbs 11:21

God doesn't always stop bad things right away, but He promises that one day, all wrongs will be made right. We might not see it today, but His fairness is always at work.

What to Remember

Even when we don't understand why God allows bad things to happen, we can trust that He is always with us. He sees the bigger picture. And even in hard times, He's working for a greater purpose.

Sometimes pain comes from people's choices, and other times it's because the world itself is broken by sin. But no matter what, God is still good. Whenever you're hurting, you can talk to Him in prayer, find comfort in His Word, and lean on others for support.

God also promises to bring justice. One day, He will make everything right. Until then, we have to remind ourselves that God is still in control, still loving, and still working for good, no matter how hard life may feel.

TALK ABOUT IT

1. When something bad happens, how can you remember that God still cares about you?

2. How does Joseph's story show you that God can bring something good out of a tough situation?

3. What's one way you can trust God when life feels hard or confusing?

Chapter 30

Why Does God Let Me Make Mistakes?

Everyone makes mistakes sometimes. It's part of being human. Maybe you've said something you wish you hadn't or made a choice that hurt someone. You might think, *If God loves me, why doesn't He stop me from messing up?* That's something a lot of people wonder about.

The Bible tells us that God loves us so much that He lets us make our own choices. Sometimes we make mistakes without meaning to, like forgetting to take out the garbage or spilling a glass of milk. Other times we choose to do what we know is wrong, like lying or taking something that doesn't belong to us. That's called sin. Mistakes happen by accident, but sin is a choice.

Even though God could stop us from doing wrong, He doesn't. Instead, He uses the choices we make to show us how deep His love and forgiveness really are.

A Story About a Wrong Choice

Jesus once told a story about a young man who made a very bad decision. He asked his father for his share of the family's money and then left home to spend it all on wild living.

Before long, he had nothing left. Hungry, ashamed, and full of regret, he knew he had messed up. So he decided to go home and apologize.

He expected his father to be angry. But instead, his father ran to him, hugged him, and welcomed him back with joy. Even though he sinned, his father never stopped loving him.

This story is called the Parable of the Lost Son, and it isn't just about a son and his father. Jesus told it to help us understand that even when we do wrong, God still loves us and wants us to come to Him. God is like the father in the story, always loving, patient, and ready to forgive.

It shows us that no matter how far we wander or how badly we mess up, God is always waiting to forgive us and help us start again. And just like the son learned a lesson from his choices, we can learn from ours too.

Learning From Mistakes

When you make a mistake, what matters most isn't what went wrong, but how you respond. Sometimes we want to hide what we did or pretend it didn't happen, but that only makes things harder. When you admit what happened, learn from it, and keep moving forward, you'll grow into a wiser and kinder person. God often uses moments like these to teach us important lessons.

Think about learning to ride a bike. You probably fell a few times before you got the hang of it. Those falls weren't fun, but they taught you how to balance and keep going. Mistakes work the same way. Each one gives us a chance to learn something new and try again.

The Bible says that when we face challenges, we can also grow in our faith. When we keep going and don't give up, our hearts become stronger too (James 1:2–4). God doesn't expect us to be perfect. He just wants us to keep growing in wisdom and trusting Him along the way.

Why God Lets Us Choose Sin

Sometimes we don't just make a mistake. We choose to sin by doing something we know is wrong.

When that happens, God doesn't stop us because He wants us to choose to obey Him on our own, not because we're forced to. If He made us always do what's right, we'd never learn how to truly love or trust Him. God lets us make our own choices, even wrong ones, because He knows we can grow from them.

When we sin, it shows how much we need God's help. He invites us to come to Him, tell Him the truth about what we did, and ask for help to change. God teaches us through our choices, helps us get back on the right path, and gives us a new start. He always forgives us when we ask, but He also wants to help our hearts grow so we'll want to do what's right the next time.

Imagine a child who tells a lie that hurts someone's feelings. Their parent might be disappointed, but their love for the child would never change. Instead, they would explain why lying is wrong, offer forgiveness, and help the child make things right. That's how God treats us. He loves us even when we fall short. Every time we come to Him, He helps us start fresh and shapes our hearts to become more like His.

What to Remember

Mistakes are a normal part of life, and sin helps remind you how much you need God. When you make mistakes, you can learn from them and keep growing. When you sin, you can turn to God, rely on His strength, and remember how much you need His grace.

God's forgiveness is always available. No matter what you've done, His mercy will never run out. God is always ready to welcome you back with open arms and a heart full of love.

TALK ABOUT IT

1. How does the story of the lost son show you what God is like when you've done something wrong?

2. What's one lesson you've learned from a mistake or sin you made in the past?

3. God shows you grace when you mess up. What are some ways you can show grace and kindness to others when they do something wrong?

Part 6

God's Plan for Life After Death

Chapter 31

What Happens When We Die?

Have you ever wondered what happens after we die? It's one of the biggest questions people ask, and it's okay to be curious. Thinking about death can feel a little scary and confusing. But the Bible tells us that God cares about our questions, and He doesn't leave us alone in our wondering. Even though we don't know everything, He gives us enough answers to fill our hearts with peace and hope.

What Happens Right After We Die?

The Bible teaches that when someone dies, their body stops working and returns to dust, becoming part of the ground again. But that's not where the story ends. We're more than just our bodies. God created each of us with a spirit. That's the special part of us that connects with Him (Ecclesiastes 12:7).

For those who follow Jesus, death is not something to be afraid of. When this life ends, our spirit leaves the body and goes to be with the Lord, where we are safe and fully alive with Him.

When Jesus was on the cross, a man being crucified next to Him also faced death that day. This man put his faith in Jesus. In response, Jesus told him:

"Truly I tell you,
today you will be with me in paradise."
— Luke 23:43

That promise shows us that everyone who trusts in Jesus is safe with Him immediately after they die.

Heaven is not just a nice idea. It's a real place. A perfect place. And God wants us to be there with Him.

God's Plan for New Life

But even Heaven is just the beginning of what God has planned. One day, Jesus will come down and gather all His followers, both those who have already died and those who are still living, to meet Him in the clouds. He will give brand-new, perfect bodies to His people. These new bodies will never get sick or feel pain again (Philippians 3:20–21).

Not only will we have new bodies, but God has even more planned for the future.

After Jesus defeats evil forever, God will create a New Heaven and a New Earth. It will be a place with no more sadness, crying, or death. God will wipe away every tear, and all the hard and painful things of this life will be gone forever (Revelation 21:4).

We can believe all of this because of what Jesus did. He died on the cross and came back to life. His resurrection proves that He has power over death and that His promises are true.

Because Jesus rose from the dead, we can trust God's promise that one day we will rise to new life too (1 Corinthians 15:20–22).

When Someone You Love Dies

Even when we know all of this, it still hurts to lose someone we love. It's normal to feel sad. God understands how we feel, and He's close to us in those painful moments.

When Jesus' friend Lazarus died, Jesus wept (John 11:35). His eyes filled with tears, and His heart ached with sorrow. That moment shows us something important. God understands our sadness, and He knows what it's like to lose someone you love.

Even when we feel broken, we can remember something beautiful. Nothing in all creation can ever separate us from God's love (Romans 8:38–39). When we turn to Him, His love holds us close and can help us through the most difficult times.

What to Remember

Because of Jesus, death is not the end. For those who love Him, it's the beginning of eternal life with God. We can trust in His love and promises, knowing that He's with us now and will never leave us.

And one day, Jesus will return and make everything new. He will bring all believers together to live with Him forever in a world filled with perfect joy, peace, and love.

TALK ABOUT IT

1. How does it make you feel to know that for everyone who trusts in Jesus, death leads to eternal life with Him?

2. When someone you love dies, what's one way you can find comfort in God's love and promises?

3. How does Jesus' resurrection give you confidence that His promises about life after death are true?

Chapter 32

What Will Heaven Be Like?

What do you picture when you think about Heaven? The Bible tells us it's more wonderful than anything we could ever dream of. Heaven is a beautiful place where everything is full of peace and love. It's where believers go after they die and are welcomed into God's glorious presence forever.

A Vision of Heaven

The Bible gives us a powerful glimpse of Heaven through a vision God gave to the apostle John. In this vision, Heaven is filled with light, beauty, and praise. Flashes of lightning burst from God's throne, along with rumblings and peals of thunder. A glowing rainbow that shines like an emerald surrounds it, and what looks like a sea of glass, clear as crystal, stretches out before it. God has the appearance of precious jewels, and heavenly creatures praise Him day and night. Elders dressed in white lay their crowns at His feet (Revelation 4:2–11).

Jesus is there, radiant with glory. He stands at the center of the throne, and millions of angels surround Him with songs of praise (Revelation 5:6–12).

While this vision doesn't fully describe what life will be like just yet, it gives us a glimpse of the majesty and worship that fills God's presence. But there's more to come.

A Forever Home on a New Earth

One day, the Heaven and Earth we know will pass away, and God will make everything new. He will create a New Heaven and a New Earth. They will be perfect, and the New Earth will never have sadness, pain, or death again. Everything broken in this world will be gone, replaced by joy, peace, and beauty beyond anything we've ever known (Revelation 21:1, 4).

When that day comes, a city called the New Jerusalem will come down from Heaven to Earth (Revelation 21:2–3). The Bible says this Holy City will shine with the glory of God. Its walls will be made of colorful gems, its gates will be giant pearls, and its streets will be gold as pure as transparent glass (Revelation 21:10–21).

This brand-new world will be our eternal home, not the current Heaven, but the New Earth where God will live with His people forever.

God's Glory and the Gifts of the Holy City

In the New Jerusalem, a beautiful river called the River of the Water of Life will flow from God's throne. On each side of the river will grow the Tree of Life, which will provide fresh fruit every month (Revelation 22:1–2). These gifts show us that in God's forever kingdom, we'll never be in need. God will take care of everything.

We also won't need the sun or moon, because God's glory will shine so brightly that it will light up everything. Jesus Himself will be the lamp for the whole city. And there will never be night again, because the light of God's presence will never fade (Revelation 21:23; 22:5).

What Will We Do in This New Creation?

Our forever home won't be boring. It will be full of life, love, music, and joy. People from every nation will gather to worship God with happy hearts and experience His love like never before (Revelation 7:9–10). There will be no fear, no pain, and no tears. Instead, we'll enjoy the comfort of being safe with God forever.

We don't know everything we'll do here, but we know it will be more amazing than anything we can imagine. God is the Creator of love, beauty, and adventure. So whatever He's preparing for us will be better than anything we could come up with on our own.

The Bible says:

> "What no eye has seen, what no ear has heard,
> and what no human mind has conceived—
> the things God has prepared for those who love him."
> — 1 Corinthians 2:9

How Can We Know We'll Be There?

Getting to Heaven isn't about being perfect or doing everything right. The Bible says the only way to Heaven is through Jesus.

Jesus said:

> "I am the way and the truth and the life.
> No one comes to the Father except through me."
> — John 14:6

If you trust in Jesus as your Lord and Savior, you can be sure that one day you'll be with Him forever.

What to Remember

Heaven is real, and the Bible gives us a stunning glimpse of it. Believers go there to be with Jesus after they die, and it's filled with joy, beauty, and worship beyond what we can fully imagine.

But one day, everything will change. God will make a New Heaven and a New Earth where everyone who belongs to Him will live with Him forever. This new creation will be full of peace, love, and adventure, and will be far greater than our wildest dreams.

Jesus is already preparing a place in Heaven for everyone who loves Him (John 14:2–3). And if you follow Jesus, you can look forward to the day when you'll be home with Him at last, completely surrounded by His never-ending love.

TALK ABOUT IT

1. What part of the Bible's description of Heaven or the New Earth excites you the most?

2. How does it make you feel to know that God is preparing a forever home where there will be no more pain, sadness, or death?

3. Why is it important to remember that the only way to Heaven is through Jesus?

Chapter 33

Will We See Our Loved Ones Again?

Have you ever missed someone so much that it made your heart ache? Maybe someone you love has passed away, like a grandparent, a friend, or even a parent or sibling. You might wonder, *Will I see them again in Heaven?* While the Bible doesn't tell us everything, it does give us strong clues that help us hold on to hope.

A Home Where We Belong

Before Jesus died, He comforted His disciples with a promise. He said that His Father's house has many rooms, and He was going there to prepare a place for them. He also promised to come back and take them to be with Him, so they could live together forever (John 14:2–3).

This shows that Heaven is real, and that Jesus is getting it ready for everyone who loves Him. If the people we love trusted in Jesus too, we can have hope that we'll be together again, where we truly belong.

The Comfort of Reunion

When writing a letter to Christians whose loved ones had passed away, the apostle Paul gave some comforting words. He said that when Jesus returns, believers who have already died will rise first. Then those still alive will join them, and we'll meet Jesus in the clouds. From that moment on, we'll be with the Lord forever (1 Thessalonians 4:16–17).

The Bible says we'll be "caught up together." That gives many Christians hope that we'll be reunited with loved ones who followed Jesus too.

When a Child Is Lost Too Soon

In the Old Testament, King David faced something heartbreaking. His baby boy became very sick. David prayed and fasted for days, begging God to heal him. But the child still died (2 Samuel 12:18–19).

Even in his sorrow, David spoke with hope. When talking about his son, he said:

> "He will not return to me,
> but I will go to him."
> — 2 Samuel 12:23

David didn't say this as a wish or a guess. He truly believed he would see his child again. He trusted that God's love is stronger than death.

Losing someone young, like a baby brother or sister, a cousin, or a friend, can hurt in a way that's hard to explain. But the Bible says that God sees every tear and stays close when we're hurting (Psalm 34:18). He understands every bit of your sadness and wants to comfort your heart.

One day, God will bring His children together again, safe and whole in His arms.

Recognizing Others in Heaven

In the Bible, there's a story where Jesus took three disciples up a mountain. As the disciples watched, Jesus' face shone brightly, and two men appeared with Him: Moses and Elijah. Moses had died long before then, and Elijah had been taken up to Heaven in a chariot of fire many years earlier (2 Kings 2:11). Even though the disciples wouldn't have known what Moses or Elijah looked like, they still recognized who they were (Matthew 17:1–3).

This story gives us a glimpse of how people may recognize each other in Heaven.

Paul shared something similar in another one of his letters:

> "Then I shall know fully,
> even as I am fully known."
> — 1 Corinthians 13:12

That verse gives many Christians hope that we will still be ourselves and be reunited with those we love.

What if I'm Not Sure They Believed?

This is a hard question, especially if someone you love has died and you don't know if they followed Jesus. If your heart feels heavy, talk to a trusted adult like a parent or pastor. It's okay to cry and ask God your questions. He understands. And even when we don't have answers, we can trust that God is always loving, always good, and always fair.

You can also pray for peace and thank God for the time you had with that person. He promises to give comfort when your heart feels broken.

What to Remember

The Bible gives us real hope that we'll see our loved ones again, as long as they belong to Jesus and we do too. Heaven is not pretend. It's a real home, full of beauty and light, and it's the beginning of forever with God.

We will be with Jesus, and the Bible gives us strong reasons to believe that reunion with those we love is part of that future.

We may not know exactly what it will be like, but we do know that God's promises are true, His love never ends, and His plans are more wonderful than anything we can imagine.

So when your heart aches for someone who is gone, remember that this life is not the end of the story. For everyone who belongs to Jesus, there is a forever future filled with peace, joy, and the beautiful hope of being together again.

TALK ABOUT IT

1. How does it make you feel to know the Bible gives us hope of seeing our loved ones again in Heaven?

2. What part of the Bible's stories about reunion, such as King David's hope for his baby or Paul's words about meeting together, encourages you the most?

3. How does Jesus' promise that His Father's house has many rooms help you trust that we'll see our loved ones again in Heaven?

Part 7

Big Spiritual Questions

Chapter 34

Why Are There Different Religions?

All over the world, people believe in different gods, follow different rules, and tell different stories about life, death, and what comes after. But if Christianity is true, why are there so many other religions?

Let's take a look at why this happens and why the message of Jesus is unlike anything else.

Searching for God

Imagine being lost in a giant maze, surrounded by others who are lost too. Some people try one path, and then another, hoping they're going the right way. Others follow a map that turns out to be wrong. Some wander in circles, confused and frustrated, while a few feel so lost they stop trying altogether.

That's what it can be like when people try to find God without knowing which path leads to Him. They search with hope in their hearts, but many end up going the wrong way.

For thousands of years, people all over the world have searched for meaning, purpose, and truth. But instead of finding the one true God, many created their own beliefs or followed ideas that led them further away from Him. Their paths might seem right at first, but they lead to dead ends, because no amount of hard work, rule-following, or good intentions can bring us to God.

But God didn't leave people without clues. The Bible says that ever since the world was created, God has shown who He is through everything He has made. When we look at the sky, the oceans, animals, and people, it all points to a powerful and loving Creator (Romans 1:19–20). God designed the world in a way that invites people to look for Him and reach out to Him, because He's never far from any of us (Acts 17:27).

Even though God gave us clues to find Him, the Bible explains why many still choose wrong paths. Romans 1:25 tells us that long ago, people turned away from the truth about God. Instead of worshiping the Creator, they began worshiping created things.

And that still happens today. Some people worship the sun, animals, or nature. Others worship money, statues, or things made by human hands. Many believe they can reach God by being good enough or doing enough good deeds. But the Bible says we can't save ourselves. Salvation means being rescued and made right with God. It's a gift from Him, not something we can earn (Ephesians 2:8–9).

We can't climb our way to Heaven, so Jesus came down to lift us up.

What Makes Christianity Different?

Christianity is different because it's not about people reaching up to God. It's about God reaching down to us.

Here are a few more reasons Christianity stands apart from every other religion:

We're Saved by Grace

Most religions teach that people must earn their way to God by doing good things or following special rules. But in Christianity, God's love does what our effort never could. We're saved simply by trusting in Jesus and accepting His gift of grace, not by anything we can do on our own.

> "He saved us,
> not because of righteous things we had done,
> but because of His mercy."
> — Titus 3:5

Jesus Conquered Death

Jesus didn't just teach nice things. He proved He is the Son of God by rising from the dead. After dying on the cross for our sins, He came back to life three days later. No one else in history has done that. His resurrection proves that His promise of eternal life is real.

The Bible Is Backed by Evidence

The Bible isn't just a book of spiritual ideas. It's grounded in real history. The words we read today match some of the oldest copies ever discovered with remarkable accuracy. When the Dead Sea Scrolls were found in 1947, scholars were amazed at how carefully the Bible had been copied and passed down over thousands of years.

Even outside the Bible, ancient sources like Josephus (a Jewish historian), Tacitus (a Roman historian), and Pliny the Younger (a Roman governor), mentioned Jesus in their records. These men weren't Christians, but their writings confirm that Jesus was a real person who lived, was crucified, and had followers who truly believed He rose from the dead. All this evidence helps us trust that the Bible is true, both spiritually and historically.

Why Does God Allow Different Religions?

If Jesus is the only way to God, why doesn't God make everyone believe in Him?

The answer is that God gives people the freedom to choose. He doesn't force anyone to love Him, because love is only true when it's given by choice.

The Bible says that when people search for God with their whole heart, they will find Him.

> "You will seek me and find me
> when you seek me with all your heart."
> — Jeremiah 29:13

But not everyone chooses to seek Him. Some reject God. Others follow false beliefs because they've never heard the truth. And some turn away from Jesus because they love their sin more than they want to live God's way (John 3:19–20).

Still, God is patient and kind. He wants everyone to know Him and discover the truth (2 Peter 3:9). That's why Christians are called to share the good news of Jesus, not with pressure or pride, but with love.

How Should Christians Treat People of Other Religions?

Even if someone believes differently, they're still made in God's image and deeply loved by Him. Jesus showed kindness to everyone, even when they didn't agree.

Here are some ways we can follow His example:

Speak the Truth with Love

Sharing our faith isn't about winning arguments. It's about helping others discover what's true. Jesus calls us to speak with love and humility. We should always be ready to talk about what we believe and do it in a gentle and respectful way (1 Peter 3:15).

Be Kind to Them

Even when people disagreed with Him, Jesus was patient and kind. Christians are called to do the same, showing kindness and building relationships that reflect God's love. Being kind doesn't mean we have to agree with false beliefs, but it does mean we should listen, speak with gentleness, and treat others the way we want to be treated.

Pray for Them

We can't change someone's heart, but God can. That's why prayer is one of the most powerful ways we can show love. When we pray for others, we're not just offering kind thoughts. We're talking to God on their behalf, and that's a big deal. We're asking their Creator to open their eyes to the truth about Jesus, soften their hearts, and help them see how much He loves them.

What to Remember

People all over the world have searched for God in different ways, but not all paths lead to Him. That's why there are so many religions, but only one leads to the truth. Christianity isn't about us working our way up to God. It's about God coming down to us.

Even when others believe differently, we can hold on to the truth with confidence. We don't need to be afraid of questions or differences. When you know what you believe and why it's true, you can share your faith with courage and joy.

And as you walk the path that leads to God, you might help someone else find their way out of the maze and discover Him too.

TALK ABOUT IT

1. Why do you think people all over the world search for God in different ways?

2. Why is it good news that we don't have to earn our way to God?

3. What's one way you can show kindness to someone who believes differently from you?

Chapter 35

What Is the Trinity?

The Trinity is one of the most mysterious parts of the Christian faith. Knowing about it helps us better understand who God is, even if we can't fully imagine everything about Him.

So what does the Trinity mean? The Bible teaches that there is only one God, but He exists as three Persons: God the Father, God the Son, and God the Holy Spirit. They are not three separate gods. They are one God in three Persons.

Getting to Know the Three Persons of God

Each Person of the Trinity is fully and completely God. They have always existed, even before the world began, because God is not limited by time or space. They each play a unique role in our lives, yet they are completely united in who they are, their power, and their purpose.

Let's take a closer look at each Person:

1. God the Father: Our Creator and Caregiver

God the Father created the heavens and the Earth (Genesis 1:1). With just His voice, He spoke light into the darkness and shaped the world with beauty and life. He placed the stars in the sky, filled the oceans with water, and formed each mountain. He designed every animal, every person, and He even made you with love and purpose.

But He didn't just create the world and walk away. He is our loving Father who watches over us, provides for us, guides us, and wants us to be close to Him. He made you not only to live in His world but also to know His love and be part of His family.

> "See what great love
> the Father has lavished on us,
> that we should be called children of God!"
> — 1 John 3:1

2. God the Son: Jesus, Our Savior

God the Son came to Earth as a Person named Jesus. Jesus is fully God and fully human. He was born as a baby, grew up, and lived among people. He traveled from town to town so He could teach crowds about God's love, perform powerful miracles, and treat each person He met with the perfect mix of kindness, honesty, and care. Through His words and actions, Jesus helped us see what God is really like.

But Jesus didn't come into our world just to teach and heal. His greatest mission was to rescue us from sin. The Bible says that "the wages of sin is death" (Romans 6:23), meaning separation from God forever. Jesus became the perfect sacrifice by giving His life on the cross, taking the punishment we deserved.

Because of Him, we can be forgiven and brought back into a close relationship with God.

> "For the Son of Man came
> to seek and to save the lost."
> — Luke 19:10

Jesus made a way for us to be with God forever. He is our Savior, our friend, and our King.

3. God the Holy Spirit: Our Helper and Guide

God the Holy Spirit is fully God, just like the Father and the Son. He's not just a force or a feeling. He's a real Person who works in people's hearts, even before they believe, to help them see their need for Jesus. And when someone gives their heart to Jesus, the Holy Spirit comes to live inside them forever (Romans 8:9).

When the Holy Spirit lives in us, He helps us grow in our faith and stay close to God. He reminds us of what the Bible says, teaches us how to live in a way that honors God, and gives us strength to make good choices. He also comforts us when we feel sad or lonely. The Holy Spirit is always with us, gently leading our hearts and reminding us that we belong to God.

You might notice the Holy Spirit working in your heart. Maybe a Bible verse comes to mind right when you need it, or you feel a strong urge to tell the truth, even when it's hard. You might feel peaceful when you pray, or feel a gentle nudge to forgive someone. These moments show that the Holy Spirit is near and helping you.

Jesus said the Holy Spirit would be our Helper, and He keeps that promise every day.

> "Do you not know that you are God's temple
> and that God's Spirit dwells in you?"
> — 1 Corinthians 3:16

How Can God Be Three in One?

God is one, but He exists as the Father, the Son, and the Holy Spirit. He is not three separate gods, and He does not take turns being different parts. Each Person of the Trinity is fully and completely God, yet they are not the same Person.

This has been one of the hardest ideas for people to understand throughout church history. Even adults and Bible scholars have spent centuries talking about it and trying to explain it carefully. The reason it's so difficult to grasp is because God is greater than we can fully wrap our minds around.

Pictures or comparisons can help us begin to understand, but no example can explain God perfectly. Every human idea falls short in some way, because nothing in creation is exactly like God.

Still, sometimes a simple picture can help us think about big ideas. A fire is one way people try to explain the Trinity.

A fire gives off flame, light, and heat. These three things are different, but you can't separate them, and they all belong to the same fire.

This example helps us understand togetherness, but God's nature is far greater than anything we can explain with words or drawings.

Even though we can't fully explain God, He has told us who He is. He is one God, but exists as three united Persons. Each Person is fully God, and they have always and will always exist together as one (Genesis 1:2; John 1:1–2, 14; John 17:5; Hebrews 9:14).

What to Remember

The Trinity helps us understand who God is and how much He loves us. God the Father made us and cares for us. Jesus, God the Son, saves us and shows us what God is like. And the Holy Spirit lives within us and helps us follow God every day.

Each Person of the Trinity is fully and completely God, and they have always existed together in perfect unity.

Even though the Trinity is a mystery we may never fully understand, it reminds us that God's nature is greater, deeper, and more wonderful than anything else in the world. He's always near, always working, and always loving us.

TALK ABOUT IT

1. Which Person of the Trinity do you feel like you understand the most right now?

2. How does it help you to know that the Father, the Son, and the Holy Spirit all work together as one God who loves you?

3. What's one way you've noticed the Holy Spirit helping or guiding you in your life?

Chapter 36

Who Is Satan and Why Is He Bad?

Have you ever heard someone talk about Satan or the Devil? Maybe you've heard about him at church, in a movie, or on TV. Sometimes people imagine him as a silly cartoon character with red skin, horns, and a pitchfork. But that's not what the Bible says. Satan is real, and he's not someone to laugh about.

He's a sneaky and dangerous enemy who tries to pull people away from God. That's why it's important to know the truth about who he is and what he does. We must take him seriously, but we never need to be afraid. God is stronger and always in control.

How Satan Turned Against God

The Bible says that God created everything, including the angels, and that everything He made was good (Colossians 1:16; Genesis 1:31). Satan wasn't always evil. He was originally one of God's angels.

But Satan's heart changed. He became proud and wanted to be like God, chasing glory that only God deserves (Isaiah

14:13–14). Because of his pride, he was cast out of Heaven, along with other angels who followed him (1 Timothy 3:6; Revelation 12:4).

Ever since then, Satan has been fighting against everything good. He tries to undo what God has done. The Bible calls him many names, like the Devil, the Tempter, the Serpent, and the Enemy, because of how he lies, tricks people, and causes harm. His goal is to turn people away from God and keep them from believing the truth about who God is and what Jesus has done for us.

Here are some of the ways Satan tries to hurt people and ruin their relationship with God:

- **He Lies to Us:** Satan twists the truth to make people believe lies. He wants them to think God doesn't love them, that they aren't valuable, or that sin isn't a big deal (John 8:44).

- **He Tempts Us to Sin:** Satan makes bad choices look fun, easy, or harmless. But sin always leads to pain, guilt, and feeling far from God (James 1:14–15).

- **He Tries to Cause Trouble:** Satan loves to break up relationships. He stirs up arguments, jealousy, and unforgiveness to tear people apart and leave them feeling angry or alone (James 3:14–16; 2 Corinthians 2:10–11).

- **He Blinds People to the Truth:** Satan tries to keep people from seeing who Jesus really is. He fills their minds with doubt and distraction so they won't believe the truth or understand how to be saved (2 Corinthians 4:4).

Satan's Limited Power

Satan may be powerful, but he's not even close to God's level. He can only do what God allows, because God rules over everything and God's power has no limits (Job 1:12).

On top of that, Jesus has already defeated Satan, and His victory can never be undone. When Jesus died on the cross and rose again, He broke the power of sin and death (Hebrews 2:14). If you belong to Jesus, you're on the winning team, and nothing can take that away.

But Satan still tries to tempt people to sin, because sin separates us from God. That's why it's so important to understand how serious sin is and how much it damages our relationship with God and others.

Why Sin Is So Serious

Sin is anything we do that goes against God's loving and wise commands. When we sin, it's like building a wall between us and God. That wall separates us from His love and goodness (Isaiah 59:2).

The Bible calls this separation "death." It doesn't just mean that our bodies will die one day. It also means being cut off from God's presence and the life He wants for us (Romans 6:23). And if someone keeps rejecting God and refuses His forgiveness, the Bible warns that after they die, they will face eternal separation from Him instead of going to Heaven.

The first place of separation is called Hell. But one day, even Hell will be thrown into another, final place of judgment called the Lake of Fire. The Lake of Fire is where everyone who has chosen to reject God will remain forever (2 Thessalonians 1:9; Revelation 20:14–15).

How Can We Resist Satan?

God gives us everything we need to stand strong against Satan's tricks. Ephesians 6:10–18 talks about putting on the Armor of God. This isn't armor you can see or touch. It's spiritual protection that helps us fight against lies, temptation, and fear.

Every part of this armor helps protect you in a different way. Let's take a look at what each piece means:

- **The Belt of Truth:** Like a belt that holds everything in place, God's truth keeps your faith steady. It helps you know what's real so you won't be fooled by the enemy.

- **The Breastplate of Righteousness:** Doing what's right protects your heart. When you follow God's ways, Satan has a harder time sneaking in with temptation.

- **The Shoes of the Gospel of Peace:** God's peace gives you strength to stand firm and share His love. When you walk in peace, fear doesn't shake you and trouble can't stop you.

- **The Shield of Faith:** Faith means trusting God even when life is hard. Like a strong shield, it blocks the lies and doubts that Satan tries to throw your way.

- **The Helmet of Salvation:** Knowing you belong to Jesus protects your mind. It helps you remember that you're saved, loved, and never alone.

- **The Sword of the Spirit:** This is the Bible. When you understand and believe what it says, you can use it like a sword to fight back against the enemy's lies.

God's armor protects us, and His Word shows us how to fight back:

> "Resist the devil,
> and he will flee from you."
> — James 4:7

When you say "No" to Satan, he has to back off. But that doesn't mean he won't try again. That's why God gives you armor to wear every day. With truth like a belt, faith like a shield, and Scripture like a sword, you can stand strong and walk closely with God, no matter how many times Satan shows up.

What to Remember

Satan is real, and he works hard to pull people away from God. But if you belong to Jesus, you never have to be afraid. Satan has never been stronger than God, and his power is limited.

Still, the battle is real. That's why God gives you everything you need to stand firm. His truth will guide you, His Spirit will help you, and His Word will protect you.

So stay close to God. Trust Him, listen to His voice, and walk with Him every day. He will never make you fight alone.

TALK ABOUT IT

1. What's one lie or trick you think Satan might use to try to fool kids your age?

2. How does it help you to know that Jesus has already defeated Satan through the cross and resurrection?

3. What's one part of the "Armor of God" you want to remember to use this week, and why?

Chapter 37

What Will Happen When Jesus Comes Back?

Jesus is coming back for us one day, just like He promised (John 14:2–3). The Bible tells us this clearly and joyfully. It doesn't say this to scare us, but to help us get ready for the most amazing moment the world has ever seen.

One day, in God's perfect timing, Jesus will return. He will not arrive quietly like He did as a baby in a manger. This time, He will appear as the powerful and victorious King He truly is. For everyone who follows Jesus, it will be a day of excitement, when every hope is fulfilled and eternity with Him begins.

Signs of His Return

Before Jesus comes back, the Bible says there will be signs that His return is getting closer. Jesus told us to watch for wars and rumors of wars, nations fighting each other, famines, and earthquakes. He explained that these things will start happening more often and become more severe as the time gets closer (Matthew 24:6–8).

The Bible also says that evil will grow stronger, love between people will fade, and many will turn away from God (Matthew 24:10–12). Lots of people will only care about themselves and money. They will be proud, disobedient to their parents, ungrateful, unholy, unloving, unforgiving, and without self-control (2 Timothy 3:1–5).

But there is good news too. The message about Jesus will finally reach people in every nation. When you see all these things happening, Jesus said you will know His return is near, right at the door (Matthew 24:14, 33).

Today, we can see many of these signs all around us, including wars in the news, natural disasters in many places, selfishness, lack of love, and the Gospel being shared across the world through TV, radio, and the internet. We don't know the exact day or hour, but each sign is a reminder that His return is getting closer and that we need to be ready to meet Him (Matthew 24:36).

The Rapture

When Jesus comes down from Heaven, life will change in an instant. The whole sky will echo with a loud shout, the voice of an archangel, and the trumpet call of God (1 Thessalonians 4:16). All of His followers will know He is here.

First, the bodies of believers who have died will be raised up and made completely new. Their spirits are already with Jesus (Luke 23:43), and in that moment, their spirits will be reunited with their resurrected bodies. These new bodies will never get sick, tired, or die again (1 Corinthians 15:52–53). Next, believers who are alive will also be changed and caught up to meet Jesus in the clouds (1 Thessalonians 4:17). This incredible event is often called the Rapture.

It will be the beginning of forever with God. There will be no more pain, no more sickness, and no more waiting. Only joy, peace, and life that never ends.

The Judgment Seat of Christ

After the Rapture, all believers will stand before Jesus at the Judgment Seat of Christ (2 Corinthians 5:10). This is not to decide whether someone goes to Heaven. Everyone there already belongs to Jesus. Their names are written in the Lamb's Book of Life, which is a special book in Heaven that contains the names of everyone who is saved (Revelation 21:27). Their sins are completely forgiven because of what He did on the cross (Romans 8:1).

Instead, this moment is about rewards. Jesus will lovingly honor His followers for the ways they lived for Him, the times they showed kindness, helped those in need, forgave, and shared the good news about Him with others (Matthew 6:20; 28:19–20). Every choice made to honor God will matter.

After this, everyone in Heaven will celebrate with Jesus at a great feast called the Marriage Supper of the Lamb (Revelation 19:6–9). It will be a joyful time of worship, reunion, and celebration. But while joy fills Heaven, those left behind on Earth will face a very different reality.

The Tribulation and Great Tribulation

Around this point in God's plan, the Bible tells us there will be a time of great trouble on Earth. This period will last for seven years and will be divided into two halves (Daniel 9:27; Revelation 11:2–3).

The first half is called the Tribulation. A powerful world leader, called the Antichrist, will rise and confirm a peace agreement with the nation of Israel and many others. He will be helped by another evil leader, called the false prophet, who will do miracles to trick people into following the Antichrist (Revelation 13:13–14).

Halfway through the seven years, the Antichrist will break the peace agreement. He will go into God's temple in Jerusalem and claim to be God himself, even though he isn't (2 Thessalonians 2:4). This will begin the second half, known as the Great Tribulation, and it will be much more dangerous (Matthew 24:21).

The Antichrist will demand to be worshiped. People will be pressured to take something called the mark of the beast, which is a special mark placed on a person's right hand or forehead. No one will be allowed to buy or sell without it (Revelation 13:16–17).

The Bible warns that anyone who takes the mark of the beast is choosing to follow the Antichrist instead of Jesus. They will face God's final judgment and be separated from Him forever (Revelation 14:9–11). Those who truly trust in Jesus will refuse the mark, even when it's very hard. God will give them the courage and strength to stay faithful (Revelation 14:12; Philippians 4:13). Even when hope feels far away, God will be in control, and His plan will keep moving toward victory. Many people will begin to trust and follow Jesus during this time.

The Second Coming

After the seven-year tribulation period, Heaven will be opened, and Jesus will come down in glory, riding on a white horse. The armies of Heaven, dressed in pure white, will follow close behind their King as He leads them into battle at a place called Armageddon (Revelation 16:16; 19:11–14, 19).

This will be a great battle against the Antichrist, the false prophet, the kings of the Earth, and their armies. They will gather their forces to fight against Jesus, but they will have no chance of winning. With just His powerful Word (Revelation 19:15, 21; Ephesians 6:17), Jesus will defeat them completely. The Antichrist and the false prophet will be thrown into the Lake of Fire forever (Revelation 19:20).

After the battle, Satan will be captured and locked away for 1,000 years, unable to tempt, trick, or harm anyone. For that entire time, Satan's influence over the world will be gone (Revelation 20:1–3).

The Millennial Reign

This begins the Millennial Reign, when Jesus will rule over the whole Earth with perfect justice and love (Revelation 20:4–6). His people will reign with Him, and help Him care for the world.

With Satan gone, he won't be able to spread lies or lead people into sin the way he does now. Though people will still make their own choices, Jesus will not let evil take control. Wolves and lambs will live together, and children will be safe even around wild animals (Isaiah 11:6–9). Nations will not fight against each other, and no one will be afraid (Micah 4:3–4). It will be a time of joy, safety, and worship of the one true King.

At the end of the 1,000 years, Satan will be released for a short time. He will make one final attempt to fight against God, but Jesus will quickly defeat him. Then Satan will be thrown into the Lake of Fire forever (Revelation 20:10). Evil will be gone for good.

The Great White Throne Judgment

Next comes the Great White Throne Judgment. This is when everyone who refused God's gift of salvation through Jesus will stand before Him. Their names will not be found in the Lamb's Book of Life, and they will be separated from God forever (Revelation 20:11–15).

This final separation will happen in the Lake of Fire, a place that even Hell will be thrown into (Revelation 20:14–15). It will be a serious and heartbreaking day.

If you belong to Jesus, you won't be part of this judgment. You will have already stood before Him at the Judgment Seat of Christ, and your place with Him is forever secure.

Some people will choose to follow Jesus during the seven-year tribulation period or during the Millennial Reign. These believers will also be saved. Their names will be written in the Lamb's Book of Life, and they will be safe with Jesus forever.

The New Heaven and New Earth

Once evil is gone, God will create a brand-new Heaven and Earth. There will be no more sin, no more death, and no more sorrow. Everything broken will be made whole (Revelation 21:1–5).

This creation will be the forever home of everyone who loves Jesus. It won't be just a copy of the world we see now. It will be better in every way, filled with beauty, peace, and purpose. And best of all, God Himself will live with His people forever.

In this new world, there will also be a special city. The Holy City, the New Jerusalem, will come down from Heaven, shining with God's glory. Its walls will sparkle with precious jewels, its streets will shine with pure gold, and God's light will fill every corner. We'll never be separated from Him again (Revelation 21:23).

The River of the Water of Life will flow from the throne of God and of the Lamb (Jesus), and beside it will grow the Tree of Life, giving fruit every month (Revelation 22:1–2). For all eternity, God will lovingly provide everything we need.

Trusting God While We Wait

The Bible doesn't tell us exactly when these events will take place (Matthew 24:36). This chapter shares one common way Christians understand the future, but faithful believers sometimes see the order and timing a little differently. Still, they all agree that Jesus is coming back. God always keeps His promises, and everyone who trusts in Jesus will be safe with Him forever.

Because of that, we don't need to be scared or confused. What matters most is doing what Jesus told us to do while we wait. He wants us to be ready and stay ready.

Here's how you can prepare your heart for Jesus' return:

- **Trust in Him as Your Savior:** Believe that Jesus died for your sins, rose from the dead, and is coming back one day. Trust Him with your heart, life, and future.

- **Talk to Him in Prayer:** Prayer is simply talking to God. You can share your thoughts, fears, and dreams with Him anytime. He's always listening.

- **Read and Obey His Word:** The Bible is God's message of love and truth. It shows us who He is and how we should live. When you read it and follow it, you grow closer to Him.

- **Live with Kindness, Love, and Hope:** When you follow Jesus, His light shines through you. When you're kind, forgiving, and full of faith, others see His love in you.

- **Stay Faithful to Him When Life Is Hard:** Some days are tough, but Jesus will never leave you. Keep trusting Him. He will always give you the strength you need.

What to Remember

God's plan for the future is filled with joy, peace, and hope for everyone who belongs to Jesus. One day, He will make everything new. Pain, sadness, and evil will be gone forever, and joy will never end (Revelation 21:4).

If you've accepted Jesus as your Savior, you have no reason to fear the future. You can look forward to it with confidence, knowing that His promises are true. You will live with Him in the perfect home He has prepared for you, safe in His care, loved beyond measure, and surrounded by everlasting beauty.

Are You Ready to Follow Jesus?

Jesus could come back at any moment. Are you ready to meet Him? Have you given your life to Him?

If not, you can make that choice right now. God loves you more than you could ever imagine, and He wants you to be with Him forever. If you believe that Jesus died for your sins and rose again, and you want to follow Him, you can pray a simple prayer like this:

Dear God,

I know I'm a sinner and need Your forgiveness. I believe Jesus is Your Son, that He died on the cross for my sins, and that You raised Him from the dead. I choose to trust Him as my Savior and follow You for the rest of my life. Please teach me to obey Your Word and fill me with Your love so I can live for You every day.

Amen.

If you prayed that prayer and meant it, the Bible says you now belong to Jesus. Your name is written in the Lamb's Book of Life, and you're part of God's family forever.

And if you haven't prayed that prayer yet, now is the time. Jesus could return at any moment, and His greatest hope is that you'll be ready. Whether you're taking your first step of faith or have followed Him for years, keep seeking Him and growing closer to Him each day. Don't wait to give Him your whole heart. He loves you, He gave His life for you, and He's coming back soon.

TALK ABOUT IT

1. How does it make you feel to know that Jesus could come back at any moment?

2. What part of God's plan for the future gives you the most hope?

3. What's one way you can live ready for Jesus' return each day?

Acknowledgements

All thanks and glory belong to God, not just for this book, but for every breath I take. He's the One who carried me through seasons when I didn't know if I would make it. He gave me strength when I had none, grace when I didn't deserve it, and direction when I couldn't see the path. This book exists because of His mercy, His timing, and His guidance. I place it in His hands, trusting Him to use it however He chooses.

To my husband, thank you for making space for me to follow the path God is unfolding before us, even when it leads us into unfamiliar territory. Your willingness to step into the unknown has meant more than words can say, and I'm grateful to walk through this life with you by my side.

To my daughters, thank you for asking the questions that sparked these pages and for reminding me what childlike faith truly looks like. I know this work often took me away from time with you, and I'm so grateful for your patience and love throughout this journey. You mean more to me than you could ever know, and I love you more than you could ever understand.

To my mom, thank you for believing in me and supporting me when I needed it most, not just through this season, but always.

To my dad, thank you for the strong foundation of faith you've always modeled. Your commitment to Jesus helped lay the groundwork for my own walk with Him.

To Mary Rue, Brandon Burns, Misty Tanner, and Ross Tanner, thank you for your time, effort, and meaningful feedback. Your input helped shape this book and gave me a fresh perspective along the way.

To Hadley, thank you for your thoughtful comment on the cover art. Your idea inspired the final design and added the perfect finishing touch.

To Lynsey Wilson, thank you for bringing this book to life with such beauty and creativity. Your illustrations capture the wonder and depth of these pages in a way words alone never could. Every detail reflects your talent and the care you poured into this project. You turned ideas into something children can step into, and I'm forever grateful for the excellence you brought to this work.

To Jennifer Spees, thank you for lending your sharp editorial eye and encouragement to this project. Your thoughtful feedback helped bring this book to completion, and I'm grateful I had the chance to work with you again.

To Pastor Mike Rue, thank you for your encouragement and support throughout this writing process. Your theological expertise has been a blessing to me. It inspired these pages and will no doubt inspire the hearts of those who read them.

To Pastor Chris Cleveland and Pastor Amber Cleveland, thank you for shepherding my family and teaching us God's Word with wisdom and grace. Your passion for sharing the

Gospel and making disciples inspires me to live with greater purpose and to help others discover the life-changing love of Jesus. Pastor Chris, thank you again to both you and Pastor Chase Replogle for your guidance and theological insight as I worked through some of these ideas.

To Pastor Nick Larson, thank you for faithfully leading our church in worship week after week and for teaching God's Word with humility and care. Your words and leadership have helped strengthen my faith, and your obedience to God's call on your life has encouraged me to follow my own. I look forward to seeing how God leads you as you step into the next chapter of your life.

To Shelley Saby, Chellney Bier, and Judy Heckel, thank you for being vessels of God's voice in moments when I needed confirmation and clarity. Your encouragement helped me finish this work with determination and perseverance.

To Alex Kempston, thank you for your leadership, patience, and support during a time of unexpected change. I know that following this calling placed an extra burden on you, and I will always be grateful for the grace you extended. Your steady example of positivity, professionalism, and integrity has left a lasting impact on my life.

And finally, to every child, parent, and reader who opens this book, if it brings you closer to Jesus, even in the smallest way, then every moment spent writing it was worth it. I pray that the truth takes root in your heart and transforms the way you see God, yourself, and the world around you.

Glossary

Abraham

A man who trusted God and became the father of the Israelites. God made a special promise to him because of his strong faith (Genesis 12:1–3).

Amen

A word said at the end of a prayer or to agree with something true. It means "so be it" or "I believe this" (2 Corinthians 1:20).

Angel

A spiritual being created by God. Angels are His messengers and sometimes protect people (Hebrews 1:14).

Anointed/Anointing

Chosen and set apart by God for a special purpose. In the Bible, oil was sometimes poured on a person's head as a sign that God had chosen them, especially kings and priests. The word can also describe someone who is led and empowered by the Holy Spirit to do God's work (1 Samuel 16:13).

Anxiety

A feeling of worry or nervousness. The Bible says we can give our worries to God because He cares for us (1 Peter 5:7).

Apologetics

Explaining and defending the Christian faith by answering questions with love and evidence. It helps people understand why Christians believe in God and the Bible (1 Peter 3:15).

Apostle

Someone Jesus chose and sent to share His message. The original twelve apostles were among Jesus' first followers. Later, others like Paul were also called apostles because God sent them to tell people about Jesus (Luke 6:13; Acts 9:15).

Apostle John

One of Jesus' disciples and apostles. He wrote several books of the Bible and was known for his deep love for Jesus and His truth.

Apostle Paul

A man who used to hurt Christians but became one of the greatest missionaries in the world after meeting Jesus. He wrote many letters in the New Testament.

Apostle Peter

One of Jesus' first followers. Even though Peter made mistakes, Jesus forgave him and used him to help lead the early church.

Archaeologist

A person who studies old objects, buildings, or tools. Many archaeologists dig things up from underground to explore places mentioned in the Bible and learn more about history.

Archaeology

The study of old things people made or used, often by digging them up from underground. It helps us understand what life was like in the past and shows that the Bible's stories really happened.

Ark

The large boat God told Noah to build to save his family and many animals from the great flood (Genesis 6:14).

Armageddon

The place where the Bible says the world's armies will gather to fight against God, but Jesus will defeat them and rule as King forever (Revelation 16:16).

Armor of God

Spiritual protection that God gives believers, like truth, righteousness, faith, and salvation, to help them stand strong against evil (Ephesians 6:10–18).

Artifact

Something made long ago, like pottery, tools, or scrolls. These items help us learn more about the events and places we read about in the Bible.

Ashamed

Feeling guilty or embarrassed about doing something wrong. When we turn to God and admit our mistakes, He forgives us and removes our shame (Psalm 34:5).

Awe

A deep sense of wonder and respect, especially when realizing how powerful, holy, and loving God is.

Balaam

A man hired to curse Israel, but God made him bless them instead. God even made Balaam's donkey speak in order to stop him (Numbers 22–24).

Baptism

A person being dipped under water and raised up again to show they have chosen to follow Jesus. It's a symbol of dying to sin and being made new through faith in Him (Romans 6:4).

Believer

Someone who believes Jesus is God's Son, trusts Him as their Savior, and chooses to follow Him.

Bible

God's true Word, written by people who were guided by the Holy Spirit. It tells of God's great love for us, His plan to save us, and how we can have a relationship with Him.

Brokenness

The hurt, sadness, or damage caused by sin in the world and in our hearts. God can heal our brokenness through His love and forgiveness (Psalm 147:3).

Character

The way a person thinks, acts, and treats others. Good character shows kindness, honesty, and faithfulness.

Chariot of Fire

A fiery, heavenly chariot that appears in the Bible as a sign of God's power. In the story of Elijah, a chariot of fire appears when God takes Elijah up to Heaven without dying (2 Kings 2:11).

Christ

A title for Jesus that means "the Anointed One" or "the Messiah." It shows that Jesus is the Savior God promised to send, the one who would rescue His people (John 20:31).

Christian

A person who believes in Jesus Christ, follows Him, and trusts Him as their Lord and Savior.

Christianity

The faith of following Jesus Christ, based on the Bible. Christianity is about having a relationship with God through Jesus, not just following rules.

Church

People who believe in Jesus and gather to worship Him, learn from the Bible, and encourage each other. The Church is God's family, but this word can also refer to the local church building where believers meet together (Ephesians 1:22–23).

Comfort

Peace, strength, and hope that God gives when we feel sad, hurt, or worried. God comforts us so that we can comfort others too (2 Corinthians 1:4).

Commandments

God's instructions for how we should live. The most famous are the Ten Commandments, which teach us to love God and love others (Exodus 20:1–17).

Compassion

Caring deeply about someone who is hurting and wanting to help them. Jesus showed compassion to many people.

Condemn/Condemnation

To declare someone guilty or deserving of punishment. The Bible says there is no condemnation for those who belong to Jesus (Romans 8:1).

Confess/Confession

To admit the truth about something we've done wrong. When we confess our sins to God, He forgives us and washes our hearts clean (1 John 1:9).

Consequence

What happens because of a choice you make, whether good or bad. God allows consequences to teach us, protect us, and guide us toward what's right.

Creation

Everything God made, including people, animals, the Earth, and the entire universe (Genesis 1:1).

Creator

Another name for God, who made the heavens, the Earth, and all living things.

Cross

The wooden beams where Jesus died to take our punishment for sin. It's now a symbol of God's love and forgiveness (1 Peter 2:24).

Crowns

Special rewards God will give in Heaven to those who loved and served Him (2 Timothy 4:8).

Crucified/Crucifixion

A painful way of death used in ancient times where a person was nailed to a wooden cross. Jesus was crucified to take the punishment for our sins, and He rose again on the third day (Luke 23:33).

David

A shepherd boy who became the king of Israel. David trusted God to help him defeat Goliath and later wrote many Psalms (1 Samuel 17:37).

Dead Sea Scrolls

Ancient scrolls found near the Dead Sea, including some of the oldest known copies of the Old Testament. They show how God's Word has been kept safe over time.

Death

When a person's body stops working. The Bible teaches that after we die, those who believe in Jesus will live forever with God, and those who reject Him will be separated from God forever (John 3:16; 2 Thessalonians 1:9).

Demon

An evil spirit that follows Satan and works against God's good plans. Demons try to deceive people, but Jesus is more powerful than all of them (Luke 4:36).

Denomination

A group of Christians who share the same beliefs and ways of worship, like Baptists or Pentecostals.

Devil

Another name for Satan, who opposes God and tries to lead people away from Him. The Devil tempts people to sin and stop trusting God (1 Peter 5:8).

Disability

A condition that makes it harder for someone to do certain things, like walking, seeing, or learning. People with disabilities are loved and valued by God (Genesis 1:27).

Disciple

A follower of Jesus. The twelve disciples mentioned in the New Testament were a group of men Jesus personally chose to travel with Him, learn from Him, and share His message with others (Matthew 4:19).

Disease

A serious illness that harms the body. Some diseases are caused by germs, but all sickness exists because the world has been broken by sin. One day, God will remove all sickness forever (Revelation 21:4).

Discouraged/Discouragement

Feeling sad or hopeless when things don't go well. God gives us hope through His Word and strength to keep going (Isaiah 40:31).

Disobey/Disobedience

Not doing what you know is right or refusing to follow God's commands.

Doubt

When you're unsure if something is true or if God really hears or cares. God understands our doubts, welcomes our questions, and helps us grow in faith (Mark 9:24).

Egypt

The country where the Israelites were once slaves until God rescued them through Moses (Exodus 20:2).

Elders

Leaders in the church who guide and care for believers.

Elijah

A prophet in the Old Testament who trusted God, boldly spoke His truth, and did miracles through God's power (1 Kings 18:36).

Enemy

Someone who tries to harm or fight against us. The Bible says our greatest enemy is Satan.

Eternal/Eternity

Lasting forever, without end. The Bible says God is eternal and promises eternal life to everyone who believes in Jesus and trusts Him as their Savior (Romans 6:23).

Esther

A brave Jewish queen in the Old Testament who saved her people from danger (Esther 4:14).

Evangelist

A person who shares the message of Jesus and helps others learn about God's love. Some evangelists travel to different places to tell people the good news about salvation through Jesus (Ephesians 4:11–12).

Evidence

Information that helps show something is true. Many kinds of evidence, like written history, fulfilled prophecies, and archaeology, help show that the Bible is trustworthy and that what it says really happened.

Faith

Trusting and believing in God, even when we can't see Him. True faith means relying on what God has said in His Word and trusting Jesus as our Savior (Hebrews 11:1).

Faithful

Always dependable and true. God is faithful to His promises (1 Corinthians 1:9).

Famine

A time when there is little or no food.

Fast/Fasted

When someone chooses not to eat food for a period of time in order to pray and depend on God for strength and guidance (Matthew 6:17–18).

False Beliefs

Ideas that go against God's truth in the Bible. Christians stay safe from false beliefs by knowing God's Word (1 John 4:1).

False Prophet

A person who pretends to speak for God but teaches lies. The Bible says to test what people say with Scripture (Matthew 7:15).

First Cause

The One who started everything. God did not come from anything else. He is the reason the universe exists and the source of all life (Genesis 1:1).

Forgiveness

Letting go of anger toward someone who has done wrong. God forgives us through Jesus when we confess our sins and say we're sorry, and He calls us to forgive others too (Ephesians 4:32).

Forsake/Forsaken

Abandoned or left alone. Jesus used this word when He cried out on the cross, carrying the weight of our sin (Matthew 27:46).

Foundation

The strong base that something is built on. The Bible says Jesus is the foundation of our faith (1 Corinthians 3:11).

Free Will

The ability God gave people to make choices. God wants us to use our free will to love Him and follow His ways. All of our choices have consequences, some good and some bad, so it's important to listen to God and try to do what's right (Deuteronomy 30:19).

Garden of Eden

The beautiful garden where the first people, Adam and Eve, lived until they disobeyed God (Genesis 2–3).

Gifts (Spiritual Gifts)

Special abilities the Holy Spirit gives believers to serve God and help others, like teaching, encouraging, or showing mercy (Romans 12:6–8).

Glory

The greatness, beauty, and power of God that makes Him worthy of praise. Sometimes God shows His glory in bright light or amazing works (Psalm 19:1).

Goliath

A giant Philistine warrior who fought against Israel. David trusted God and defeated Goliath with only a slingshot and a stone (1 Samuel 17:1–50).

God

The one true Creator of everything. He is eternal, all-powerful, and perfectly loving (Psalm 90:2).

Good News

Another name for the Gospel, which is the message that Jesus died for our sins and rose again so we can have eternal life.

Gospel

The message of salvation through Jesus Christ. The Gospel is called "the good news" because it tells us about God's love and forgiveness (1 Corinthians 15:1–4).

Grace

God's free gift of love and forgiveness that we don't earn or deserve. Through grace, we are saved by faith in Jesus (Ephesians 2:8–9).

Great Commission

Jesus' command to His followers to go into the world, share the Gospel, and make disciples (Matthew 28:19–20).

Great Tribulation

A future time of very great trouble and suffering before Jesus returns as King (Matthew 24:21).

Great White Throne Judgment

The final judgment when God will judge all who rejected Him (Revelation 20:11–15). Jesus' followers will not face this judgment.

Guide/Guidance

Direction or help in knowing what to do. God guides His people through the Bible, prayer, and the Holy Spirit (Psalm 32:8).

Guilt

The heavy feeling of knowing we did something wrong. God removes our guilt when we confess our sins and receive His forgiveness (Psalm 32:5).

Healing

When God makes someone well again, either right away or over time (Psalm 103:2–3).

Heaven

The perfect home of God, where believers go after they die to be with Him. One day, God will make a New Heaven and New Earth, and His people will live with Him there forever (Revelation 21:1–4).

Hell

A terrible place of separation from God for those who reject Him. The Bible describes it as a place of sorrow and regret, where people are punished and separated from God's presence (Luke 13:28; 2 Thessalonians 1:9).

Helper

Someone who gives aid or support. The Bible calls the Holy Spirit our Helper because He gives us strength and guidance (John 14:26).

Hezekiah

A king of Judah who trusted God and led the people back to worshiping God after they had turned away from Him (2 Kings 18:5–6).

Historian

A person who studies and writes about past events. Historians help us understand what life was like in ancient times.

Holy

Pure, perfect, and set apart. Only God is completely holy, and He calls His people to live holy lives too (1 Peter 1:15–16).

Holy City

A name the Bible gives to Jerusalem, and also to the New Jerusalem that God will bring down from Heaven when He creates the New Heaven and New Earth (Revelation 21:2).

Holy Spirit

The third Person of the Trinity. The Holy Spirit lives in believers, guiding, comforting, and giving them power to follow Jesus (John 14:26; Acts 1:8).

Humble/Humility

Not thinking of yourself as better than others, but showing kindness and respect.

Idols

Anything people put before God or worship instead of Him. The Bible warns against idols because only God deserves our worship (Exodus 20:3–4).

Image

A likeness or picture of something. People are made in the image of God, which means we are created to reflect His character (Genesis 1:27).

Inspired

Guided by God. The Bible was written by people who were inspired by the Holy Spirit, so every word is God's truth (2 Timothy 3:16).

Interpret

To interpret something means to explain or understand what it means. People sometimes interpret the same thing in different ways.

Isaiah

A prophet in the Old Testament who spoke God's messages and shared promises about the coming of Jesus (Isaiah 7:14; 9:6).

Israel/Israelites

The nation that came from Abraham's family through Isaac and Jacob, whom God renamed Israel (Genesis 32:28). The Israelites were the people who descended from Jacob's family. His 12 sons became the 12 tribes of Israel, and from this family line, Jesus was born (Genesis 35:10–12).

Isaac

The son God promised to Abraham and Sarah. Through Isaac, God continued His covenant that led to the Israelites and Jesus (Genesis 17:19).

Jacob

The son of Isaac and grandson of Abraham. God changed Jacob's name to Israel, and his 12 sons became the 12 tribes of Israel (Genesis 32:28).

Jericho

A city in the Bible whose walls fell down after the Israelites marched around it as God commanded (Joshua 6).

Jesus

The Son of God and Savior of the world. Jesus came to Earth, lived a sinless life, died on the cross for our sins, and rose again so we can have eternal life (John 3:16).

Jews/Jewish

God's chosen people in the Old Testament, also called Hebrews or Israelites (Deuteronomy 7:6). The name "Jew" comes from the tribe of Judah, which was one of the twelve tribes of Israel. Jesus was born a Jew, and through the Jewish people God carried out His plan of salvation for the world.

Jordan

A country in the Middle East, located east of Israel.

Jordan River

A river that flows between Israel and Jordan. God's people crossed it to enter the land He promised, and Jesus was baptized there (Joshua 3; Matthew 3:13–17).

Joseph

The son of Jacob who was sold into slavery in Egypt. God raised Joseph to power so he could save many people during a famine (Genesis 37–50).

Judea

The southern part of Israel where Jerusalem is located. Many important events in Jesus' life took place there.

Judge/Judgment

A judge makes decisions about what's right and wrong. The Bible also talks about God's judgment, when He holds people accountable for their choices (Romans 14:12).

Judgment Seat of Christ

The time when Jesus will reward believers for how they lived to honor Him (2 Corinthians 5:10). It's not a judgment for sin, because believers are already forgiven through Jesus. This is also called the *Bema Seat of Christ*.

Justice

Treating people in a way that is fair and right. The Bible teaches that God is just and calls His people to live that way too (Micah 6:8).

King

A ruler over a land or group of people. The Bible calls Jesus the King of kings because He rules over all (1 Timothy 6:15).

Kingdom

A land or group of people ruled by a king. The Kingdom of God means His rule over the hearts of those who follow Jesus and one day over the whole world (Luke 17:21; Daniel 2:44).

Lake of Fire

The eternal place of punishment where Satan and all who reject God will be sent after the final judgment (Revelation 20:10–15).

Lamb

A young sheep. In the Old Testament, lambs were sometimes offered to God as a sacrifice for people's sins. The Bible calls Jesus the Lamb of God because He gave His life as the perfect sacrifice for our sins (John 1:29).

Lamb's Book of Life

A book the Bible says belongs to Jesus, listing the names of those who belong to Him and will live with God forever (Revelation 21:27).

Law

The commands God gave to show His people how to live, including the Ten Commandments given to Moses (Exodus 20:1–17).

Lazarus

A friend of Jesus whom He raised from the dead to show God's power (John 11:38–44).

Lord

A title that means master or ruler. Calling Jesus "Lord" means recognizing Him as God (Philippians 2:11).

Love

Deep care and commitment toward someone. The Bible says God is love, and He calls us to love Him and love others (1 John 4:8; Matthew 22:37–39).

Manna

The special bread God provided for the Israelites in the wilderness (Exodus 16).

Marriage Supper of the Lamb

A great celebration in Heaven when Jesus will be united with His people, like a joyful wedding feast (Revelation 19:9).

Mercy

God's kindness in not giving us the punishment we deserve for our sins. He also calls us to show mercy to others (Luke 6:36).

Messiah

A word that means "the Anointed One." In the Old Testament, God promised to send the Messiah to save His people. In the New Testament, we learn that Jesus is the Messiah, also called the Christ (John 4:25–26).

Michael

An archangel mentioned in the Bible who serves and obeys God. Michael is described as a powerful angel who fights against evil (Jude 1:9; Revelation 12:7).

Millennial Reign

The future time the Bible describes when Jesus will rule as King over the Earth for 1,000 years (Revelation 20:4).

Miracle

An amazing event that shows God's power, like healing the sick, calming a storm, or raising the dead. Miracles show us that nothing is impossible for God (Acts 2:22).

Missionary/Missionaries

A missionary is a follower of Jesus who goes out to share the Gospel and show God's love to others, sometimes in places far from home (Matthew 28:19).

Mock/Mocked

To make fun of someone in a mean way. Jesus was mocked before He was crucified, but He did not fight back (Matthew 27:31).

Moses

A leader chosen by God to rescue the Israelites from slavery in Egypt (Exodus 3:10). God gave Moses the Ten Commandments on Mount Sinai (Exodus 31:18).

Mount Sinai

The mountain where God gave Moses the Ten Commandments and made a special promise to the Israelites (Exodus 19:20).

Mourn/Mourning

Deep sadness over losing someone or something. The Bible says God comforts those who mourn (Matthew 5:4).

New Heaven and New Earth

The perfect home God will make when sin and death are gone. Everyone who trusts in Jesus will live with Him there forever (Revelation 21:1–5).

New Testament

The second part of the Bible, written after Jesus came to Earth. It tells about His life, death, and resurrection, and how His followers shared the Gospel and began the first churches.

Noah

A man who trusted God and built a huge boat called an ark. God used Noah to save his family and many animals during a worldwide flood (Genesis 6–9).

Obey/Obedience

Listening carefully and doing what you're told. In the Bible, obedience means following God's commands because we love and trust Him (John 14:15).

Old Testament

The first part of the Bible, written before Jesus came to Earth. It tells about God's creation, His promises, His laws, and the history of Israel.

Parable

A simple story Jesus told to teach something important about God and His Kingdom (Matthew 13:34).

Pastor

A church leader who teaches God's Word, cares for the people, and helps them grow in faith (1 Peter 5:2).

Persecution

Being treated badly or harmed because of what you believe. Jesus warned His followers that they would face persecution (John 15:20).

Pontius Pilate

The Roman governor of Judea who allowed Jesus to be crucified, even though he knew Jesus was innocent (Matthew 27:24).

Praise

Words, songs, or actions that show love, thankfulness, and honor to God (Psalm 150:6).

Prayer

Talking and listening to God. Prayer can include thanking Him, asking for help, confessing sins, and worshiping Him (Philippians 4:6).

Prophet

A person chosen by God to speak His message to others. God promised to raise up prophets to guide His people (Deuteronomy 18:18).

Prophecy/Prophecies

A message from God, sometimes about what will happen in the future, spoken through a prophet (2 Peter 1:21).

Psalm

A song or poem that expresses love, thanks, or prayers to God. The Bible's book of Psalms includes 150 of them.

Rapture

When Jesus comes back to take believers to Heaven. It will happen suddenly, as Christians who have died and those still alive are gathered to meet Him in the clouds (1 Thessalonians 4:16–17).

Red Sea

The sea God parted so the Israelites could escape from Egypt on dry ground. When the Egyptian army tried to follow, the waters came back and covered them (Exodus 14).

Religion

A system of beliefs and practices about God or gods. Christianity is different from other religions because it's not just about rules, but about a real relationship with the One who created you (Jeremiah 9:23–24).

Repent/Repentance

Turning away from sin and turning back to God. Repentance means being truly sorry for wrong choices and choosing to follow Him instead (Acts 3:19).

Resurrection

Coming back to life after death. Jesus' resurrection proved His power over sin and death, and one day all believers will be raised to eternal life (1 Corinthians 15:20–22).

Reverence

A deep respect and honor for God. To show reverence is to treat Him as holy and worthy of worship (Hebrews 12:28).

Rewards (God's Rewards)

Blessings God promises to give His children for living in a way that honors Him. These rewards are given in Heaven and will last forever (Matthew 6:20).

Righteous/Righteousness

Being right with God and living in a way that pleases Him. We are made righteous through faith in Jesus, not by our own good works (Romans 3:22).

River of the Water of Life

A bright, clear river flowing from the throne of God and of the Lamb in the New Jerusalem. It shows God's eternal goodness and care for His people (Revelation 22:1–2).

Sabbath

A special day of rest and worship. God created the Sabbath so people could pause from work, spend time with Him, and be refreshed (Exodus 20:8–10).

Sacred

Something holy and set apart for God.

Sacrifice

Giving up something valuable to show love or obedience to God. In the Old Testament, people offered animals as sacrifices for sin, but Jesus became the final sacrifice for all sin when He died on the cross (Hebrews 10:10).

Salvation

The gift of being rescued from sin and given eternal life with God through faith in Jesus (Ephesians 2:8).

Samuel

A prophet and judge in Israel who listened to God's voice and guided the people. God told Samuel whom to anoint as king (1 Samuel 7:15–17; 10:1; 16:1).

Satan

A fallen angel who rebelled against God and became the ruler of demons. He tries to trick people into sin. Satan is not equal to God and can only do what God allows. One day, God will defeat him forever (Revelation 20:10).

Savior

Another name for Jesus, who saves people from their sins (Matthew 1:21).

Scholar

A person who studies and teaches about an important subject, such as the Bible.

Scripture

Another word for the Bible, God's written Word (2 Timothy 3:16).

Scribe

A person who carefully copied God's Word so it could be preserved and shared with others.

Second Coming

When Jesus returns to Earth in power and glory to rule as King (Revelation 19:11–16).

Serve/Service

Using our time and talents to help others, as a way to honor God (Galatians 5:13).

Shepherd

A person who takes care of sheep. The Bible calls Jesus the Good Shepherd because He lovingly cares for and protects His people (John 10:11).

Signs

Special events or miracles that show God's power and help people believe in Him (John 20:30–31).

Sin

Anything we think, say, or do that disobeys God. All people have sinned and need His forgiveness (Romans 3:23).

Sinless

Never doing anything wrong or against God. Only Jesus lived a sinless life (Hebrews 4:15).

Slavery

When people are forced to live and work without freedom. The Bible tells how God freed the Israelites from slavery in Egypt (Exodus 12–14).

Spirit

The part of a person that lives forever. The Holy Spirit is God's Spirit who lives in believers and helps them follow God (Romans 8:11).

Staff

A long stick carried by shepherds to guide and protect their sheep.

Tax Collector

A person who collects taxes or money for the government. In ancient times, they were often disliked because many of them cheated people.

Temple

A holy place connected to God's presence. In the Bible, the temple in Jerusalem was a special building where God was worshiped. The Bible also speaks about a temple connected to future events. The bodies of believers are God's temple too because the Holy Spirit lives in them (1 Corinthians 6:19; 2 Thessalonians 2:4).

Tempt/Temptation

The feeling or desire to do something wrong or against God's will. Jesus was tempted but never sinned (Matthew 4:1–11).

Ten Commandments

Ten important laws God gave to Moses on Mount Sinai to teach His people how to love Him and love others (Exodus 20:1–17).

Throne

A special chair where a king sits to rule. In the Bible, God's throne represents His power and rule over everything (Psalm 103:19).

Tomb

A place where people are buried. Jesus was placed in a tomb after He died, but He rose from it three days later (Matthew 28:1–6).

Tradition

Something people do in a special way because it has been passed down over time. Churches sometimes have different traditions, like how they worship or practice baptism.

Translation/Translators

The Bible was first written in Hebrew, Aramaic, and Greek. When it's translated, it's written in another language so more people can read it. Translators are the people who do this work.

Tree of Life

A tree described in the Bible that gives life from God. It was in the Garden of Eden and will also be in the New Jerusalem, giving fruit each month and leaves for healing (Genesis 2:9; Revelation 22:2).

Tribulation

A time of great difficulty, trouble, or suffering. The Bible also uses this word for a future time of great distress on Earth that will take place before Jesus' Second Coming (Matthew 24:21).

Trinity

There is one God who exists as three Persons: God the Father, God the Son (Jesus), and God the Holy Spirit (Matthew 28:19).

Trust

Believing that someone is true and reliable. Trusting God means depending on Him completely and knowing He always keeps His promises (Proverbs 3:5).

Unrighteousness

Living in a way that does not please God. It's the opposite of righteousness (Romans 1:18).

Wages

The payment someone earns for their work. The Bible says the wages of sin is death, but God gives the free gift of eternal life through faith in Jesus (Romans 6:23).

Weary

Feeling physically or mentally exhausted, especially from hard work or carrying heavy burdens. God promises to give strength to the weary (Isaiah 40:29).

Wicked

Doing evil or turning against God. The wicked choose to follow sin instead of Him (Psalm 1:6).

Wilderness

A dry, empty, or wild place. God's people often traveled through the wilderness, and Jesus spent time there too (Deuteronomy 8:2).

Wisdom

Understanding what's right and making good choices. True wisdom comes from God (Proverbs 2:6).

Word of God

Another name for the Bible. It's God's message to people, showing us His truth and love (Hebrews 4:12).

Worship

Showing love, honor, and thanks to God through prayer, songs, and how we live (Psalm 95:6).

About the Author

Jackie Burns is a Christian author with a passion for apologetics and a heart for helping kids build a rock-solid foundation of faith. After building her career in the corporate world, Jackie felt God calling her to leave it all behind and follow Him into something new. Following His lead, she walked away and devoted her time to finishing *The Wondering Place*, the book He had placed on her heart. What began as an act of obedience became a journey of trust, purpose, and growth.

The idea for *The Wondering Place* began when her daughter asked, "Why do we have to be punished for something Adam and Eve did?" Jackie realized she didn't have a simple, child-friendly way to explain it. That tender moment opened her eyes to a larger issue. Kids are asking big theological questions, and parents often feel unprepared to respond. In moments like these, children deserve clear, biblical answers they can understand and rely on.

Jackie believes many of today's youth, even some from Christian homes, are drifting into confusion, anxiety, and unbelief because they were never given a solid foundation of truth to stand on. From her own experience, she understands the impact that clear, evidence-based facts about God can have on someone's life. She hopes this book will help children grow in confidence, deepen their faith, and walk continuously with Jesus. Not through blind faith, but through understanding, reason, and a relationship with the Lord that will last a lifetime.

Jackie lives in Minnesota with her family. She loves being at church, where gathered worship, Bible study, and fellowship with other Jesus followers renew her heart each week. Her home is lively and full of silliness, noise, family game nights, and too much coffee. But at the heart of it all is her love for God and the family He's blessed her with. She enjoys prayer walks outdoors, reading theology books, weaving Christian art, and finding small ways to bring God's beauty and peace into the middle of everyday chaos.